# ESSAY ON
# THE CRAFT OF
# 'CELLO-PLAYING

## VOLUME 2

*The Left Hand*

# ESSAY ON THE CRAFT OF 'CELLO-PLAYING

## VOLUME 2

### *The Left Hand*

CHRISTOPHER BUNTING

**Sangeeta Publications**
15 Queens Road, London W5 2SA, UK.

PUBLISHED BY SANGEETA PUBLICATIONS
15 Queens Road, London W5 2SA, UK.

First published in 1982 by Cambridge University Press

British Library Cataloguing in Publication Data
A Catalogue record of this book is available from the British Library

Volume 2          ISBN  0-9527902-3-8          ISMN  M-9002002-4-2

Cover drawing by Christopher Bunting

Printed by Intype London Ltd.
Elm Grove, Wimbledon, London SW19 4HE

To
# KENNETH LAMBERT
with admiration, affection, and gratitude

# Contents

# Development of the Kinetic Touch, and first thoughts about finger independence

One of the main problems in the left-hand technique of the 'cello is that of clarity of enunciation. This is because of the thickness of the strings and the large amount of air and wood that has to be set into vibration with each note. It is a problem of inertia.

The ideal finger-action to achieve this clarity is intimately bound up with the factors we have thought about in the Prelude (volume 1). The finger must be raised as if tensioning a spring so that there is a progressively restoring force proportionate to the distance away from the string. At a certain point, that of maximum tension, a *decision* is taken suddenly to release the muscles that are opposing this restoration of the finger to its point of rest on the string. It is here that we shall see the application of the Zen principle; we see the 'negative' aspect of the taking of a positive decision, the decision to play a note. One might say that instead of 'playing-the-note', we suddenly stop 'not-playing-it!' When the tension is released, the finger flies down towards the string unimpededly, and, because of the rapidity of this action, will carry the string with it on the short distance from its point of rest to contact with the fingerboard. The clarity of articulation is related to the *acceleration* of the finger from the 'let-go' point to the point where it hits the string. Thus there is even hope for the little finger!

As with tennis, it is the follow-through which is important because, curiously, it is the knowledge that one is going to follow through (imaginatively) which lends confidence to the initial release. If there is the slightest worry about intonation, there is likely to be an inhibition of this free fall of the finger. It is vital to develop the ability to tension one finger independently, whilst allowing the other fingers to remain relaxed. Indeed, this is the story throughout: we are studying the whole shifting palette of tensions and relaxations, both in the grosser sense of the body posture and the local sense of finger activity.

From cybernetics we know that a decision is of the yes or no variety, 'on' or 'off', and not *qualitative*. I believe that it is the prevalent idea of a qualitative decision in finger action that leads to much muddled playing.

## Development of Independence

We might liken the action of one finger to the action of the 'big-end' in a car engine. As it rises with the piston to the top of the cylinder, it compresses the gas. Then the spark ignites the gas, this corresponding with the 'decision' spoken of above, and this energy is released into motion, the flywheel carrying it round to the next phase of the cycle. Therefore, we can liken our four fingers to the four pistons of a car engine, each going through a different stage in the cycle, so that one finger has just relaxed having played, another one is getting ready and is at the tensioning phase. Of course, the metaphor breaks down eventually, because the order of firing, so to speak, is seldom the same. Just as I have introduced the idea of *differentiation of function*, I would now like to introduce the idea of the *'elimination, or, at least, reduction, of pattern preference'.* I have come to feel that this is one of the most important aspects of our studies.

Alfred Cortot, in his *Principes Rationnels de la Technique Pianistique*, has a section which would seem to be orientated towards this end. One might liken it to the cleaning and preparing of a canvas by an artist so that he has a completely white and featureless background upon which he may then employ whatever artistic gestures he may wish. I would like this concept to be a thread running through all our studies, that they should lead to a conscious control of what we wish to achieve.

I believe that from the earliest experiences our fingers acquire certain 'preferences'. A favourite tune or perhaps the first tune we ever studied, tends to remain 'in' the fingers, and if later we want to play something that is almost, but not quite, similar to it, there is a conflict of orders coming down to the fingers from the brain, leading to confusion.

I shall later have a great deal to say about mental planning and practising, but the reader may immediately satisfy himself of the force of this, if he will *mentally* practise the scale of C major, for instance, ten times with one note wrong and then attempt to play the same scale correctly on the instrument. The result is disturbing.

It is said that 'one showing is worth a thousand sayings'. In speaking of the technique of the left hand I am hindered in my inability to control the timing of your reading of this book. In teaching, ideally one controls carefully the point at which an idea is proposed, whereas here the apparent paradoxes and contradictions may assume an undue importance.

Thus if I speak at one point of action of the fingers without involving movement of the hand I urge patience, for, of course, suitable 'choreographic' movements of the hand are of the essence in deploying a phrase through different positions, and across the strings.

Most 'cellists of some competence can play a cantabile melody with fluency and, in one sense, it is not my business to interfere with this, because the result is what matters, and the very variety of means employed make the essential and valuable distinction between one person's playing and another's.

The difficulty is that a gesture of the hand that gives character to a slow phrase, may be employed as a *compensation* in a fast one. This is the bugbear. Players 'help' out an undeveloped finger with a twist or throw of the hand and this masks the problem and, becoming habitual, prevents the solution. Worse yet! They then 'practise hard' at a rapid passage with increasing tension usually with unsatisfactory results. This is what F. M. Alexander called 'end-gaining', and it violates a principle which is the only true secret of virtuosity – differentiation of function. By this I mean that one must arrive at a point, by examining the effect of the mental attitude on the physical performance and by systematic training, where each limb that makes up the total may play its part with the minimum of interference with and from other limbs. In a smoothly running industry or army each member performs his specific function in a harmonious hierarchy. A bad general, suffering from a rush of 'democratic' ideas to the head, will be found in the front line distributing comforts to the troops when suddenly he is informed of a breakthrough on the left flank and, being away from his map-table and chain of command, is unable to save those same troops from disaster.

How often does one see a 'cellist whose head is attempting to usurp the functions of 'doing' and is thus debarred from exercising the supervisory and integrative function essential for harmonious and balanced action? The private soldiers in our army are the phalanges of the fingers: let them attend to their specific function. The fingers and thumb are the corporals. Sergeant Hand has a platoon of five sections and controls them calmly, acting upon orders from above. Upper arm and forearm are lieutenants supervised by Colonel Arm, who will see to it that the chain of command is kept open (free joints) and that 'total' orders are interpreted adaptively to meet local conditions. (When we come to consider 'velocity', and its impediments, we shall discover that orders get scrambled when the joints are rigid.) Major Left-Shoulder is of balanced disposition and acts in close liaison with Major Right-Shoulder, under the supervision of Major-Gen. Neck. Over all presides General Head, sometimes accused of excessive detachment, but cool in a crisis and known for the clarity of his orders – the first of which is that none of his officers shall usurp the rôle of another.

Specifically, we do *not* tense up the whole hand in the hope that some of the tension will get where it is needed, rather on the principle of the blunderbuss, but study how to tense and release specific finger muscles sequentially, more on the focussed principle of the rifle.

The essence of the true ego is flexibility – balancing 'intention' with reality-feedback. By this I mean that the mental kinaesthetic rehearsal which precedes the action by however short an interval must be accurately attuned to the job in hand – to what is *possible*. This is axiomatic to the point of banality, but it needs to be said, for it is precisely here that lies the difficulty for so many players. Attention paid to this saves many hours of fruitless labour. This interplay of intention and reality-feedback permits a *true* integration of all the partial and asymmetric movements that make up 'cello-playing.

Surely we have all experienced a surge of good playing when 'not caring' for some reason, whether it be because one has not practised for a while and is not yet 'trying' (!) or playing something *à l'improviste* with the 'excuse' this provides – or, indeed, when lightly inebriated!

Most of us dismiss this as a freak of experience instead of cherishing it as a valuable clue. We achieve momentarily a remission of the 'trying' attitude and permit differentiation of function together with a true relaxed total integration.

Thus we must divide our examination of left-hand technique into phases, trusting that if the basic elements are sound there will be no need for misguided efforts.

# *Phase 1.*

# *Establishment of the Kinetic Touch*

What is an important but easily manageable problem for the singer with his consonants and vowels, for the pianist with his little hammers, for the violinist with his little strings and small resonating volume, becomes for the 'cellist a major concern. I refer to the question of clarity of enunciation.

For every note, we have to set into vibration large strings and large amounts of wood and air. The quality of the left-hand finger-action becomes crucial.

I use the term 'Kinetic Touch' to identify this quality of action, because it suggests a falling on to the note, a release from a spring, the energy of momentum of a body in rapid motion, in this case the distal phalanx — that portion from the furthest joint (from the palm) to the fingertip.

This quality of action is not easy for some, and so I discuss it fully, at the risk of boring those for whom it is axiomatic and incontrovertibly correct.

I am convinced that the whole of one's mind, one's *Weltanschauung*, one's 'programming', if you will, has a direct bearing on one's ability to acquire this kinetic touch and indeed on one's ability to see the need for it!

I have reservations about Zen Buddhism and its relation to the ego; I nevertheless urge you to read *Zen in the Art of Archery* by Eugen Herrigel which has become a little classic in its way. In it is suggested the quality of action that I would wish for our left-hand fingers. Norbert Wiener's books on cybernetics say the same thing in a scientific way.

'Yes, but how about those natural players', you may object, 'they haven't had to think all this out?' Well, the sad fact is that a strong intellect inhabiting a weak ego will often interfere with the instinctual processes. 'Leading with the brain' is as dangerous as 'leading with the chin', and is a disease now universally rampant. We have, if we are not natural, or, as more often happens, have ceased to be natural, to see what the situation is and at what point a wrong attitude to 'doing' may mess things up.

When we raise the finger away from the string the tension should increase (in that finger only and not the others), as if a spring were being coiled. All the finger joints contribute to this flexing until the finger resembles the leg of a prancing horse, the distal phalanx being aimed at the note. Then the finger is released to fly to the note.

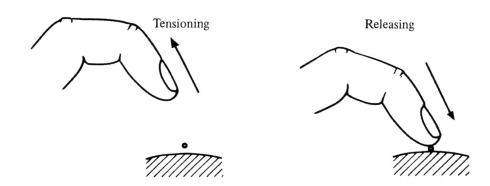

Tensioning       Releasing

The path of the distal phalanx, our hammerhead, is more or less straight. All the joints release so that when the string is reached the finger is still curved, but the radius of this curve is greater than that of the finger in the tensed position. I use the word 'position' reluctantly and only relating to a slow-motion breakdown of the action. In fact the tensing and releasing must be all part of a smooth, graceful, cyclic action. I believe that if 'Nature abhors a vacuum' she also abhors stasis. Muscles like to be used; they will tolerate neither prolonged tension nor prolonged disuse.

The decision to 'play' the note is in effect a decision to stop tensing the finger or in other words a decision to stop not playing the note! I repeat: it is a decision to stop not playing the note.

Assuming now that we have hit upon the knack of deciding to stop holding the finger away from the note *without disturbing or involving any other part of the body, or disturbing the breathing*, there still remains an impediment. The trouble is that we wish to play in tune. We wish to hit the note fair and square. If there is a doubt that this will be so, there is sometimes a check in the free flight of the finger to the string. This is most frequently present in those players that are substituting 'conscious' intonation control for a true confidence based on progressive refinement of errors, as I shall describe.

Again we encounter the habit of compensating for inadequate training and skill by misguided effort.

If one finds oneself in a bus going the wrong way it is useless and poignant to invoke the virtues of perseverance and constancy. *Il faut reculer pour mieux sauter*! Or, as F. M. Alexander put it – cease 'end-gaining' and study the precise nature of the goal to be achieved and the means whereby this may be accomplished. Stop 'trying' and study the whole psychophysical mechanism. I do not exaggerate when I say that years may be saved in this way. I have seen people shoot ahead in their development when they have started to work in this way, but it does postulate a stout heart and a modicum of intelligence, for it runs counter to the 'grain' of our training. 'Take pains', they say. 'Take trouble', they say. Why should we? Are we saints aspiring to the Higher Life through mortification? If it worked, I'd be all for it, but it does not!

Of course it is possible that those of adequate endowment in the cerebrum, brought to a point of exhaustion by many hours of frustrating labour, may spot the possibility of better use-of-the-self, all other courses having been defeated. This is probably the only justification for such prolonged agony. It strikes me as uneconomical, especially for the player who has not the time to spare and if he had would rather spend it enlarging his repertoire.

The principle of 'divide and conquer' is helpful. Study the finger action without any attempt to play in tune. I am confident that when you have had a sufficient number of successes in this, the very 'rightness' and ease of it will reinforce the habit and extirpate any temptation to return to snatching, grasping and locking.

# *Intonation (preliminary)*

I have just suggested laying on one side, for the moment, the question of intonation, in order not to impede the 'careless' fall of the finger.

I think this is the moment to clarify what is really happening when we play in tune, so that good intonation may the sooner be reintegrated into the playing.

What I shall describe will offend the puritan and the perfectionist but I am not saying what *should* be so but what *is* so. Fighting realities produces useless tension, and impedes progress.

Consider a fairly competent player. He wishes to strike C on the A string with his second finger. The experience he has had will form a kinaesthetic 'image' of the procedure. The result will be more or less close to the 261.5 cycles per second that will satisfy his ear. Any discrepancy will be fed back into the planning phase. Frequent repetitions will refine the error until it is within tolerable limits. The point to understand is that there must and will be a margin of error. The perfectionist, in his crass stupidity, will deny this. (See volume 1, p. 7.)

The human machine – if you will accept an unlovely term – controls and orders its behaviour on a feedback principle: information from the post-action phase is fed back into the planning phase. Interference with this process is disastrous, as we have seen in the Prelude in volume 1. One cannot have *exactly* 261.5 cycles per second *and* freely falling fingers!

It would be fun to mount a perfectionist on a bicycle whose front wheel has been locked into the straight-ahead position. The perfectionist denies that straight-ahead steering on a bicycle demands constant and subtle corrections. Let us hope that he is adequately insured!

# *Kinetic Touch (practical)*

But now it is time to get down to work. We have given ourselves to the chair, the spine is released, the shoulders are low-floating and the mind has been cleansed of perfectionism.

The hand is roughly at right angles to the string, the elbow very slightly lower than the hand and the fingers are slightly curved. The pad of the thumb rests lightly on the neck of the instrument and with the first finger makes a large C shape. The fingers will strike the strings at right angles (looked at from above) to the strings in the 'lower' positions.

Raise the second finger, increasing the tension as the finger retreats from the string. At the top of the movement let it go, freely falling on to F on the D string:

*Ex. 1*

Now once again. The upward, tensing movement blends into the downward, releasing flight. Let the finger fall as if about to go right through the string and the fingerboard, rather like the 'follow-through' in tennis or golf. When there is time, i.e. in a longish note (as here), the initial strike is 'backed-up' by weight deployed from the left arm (having been released from the arm/shoulder joint).

If you're out of tune or miss the string altogether do not ruin everything by self-castigation, just file the error away. Above all, do *not* put it right. The aim is not to acquire the skill of '*putting*-things-right' but of '*getting*-things-right'. 'Putting-things-right' does have a rôle to play in 'cello-technique, but it is an emergency procedure and we don't want to develop our craft by way of emergency measures!

Here is the full exercise – to be performed daily at the beginning of the practising session (left hand only, no bow).

*Percussion 1a*

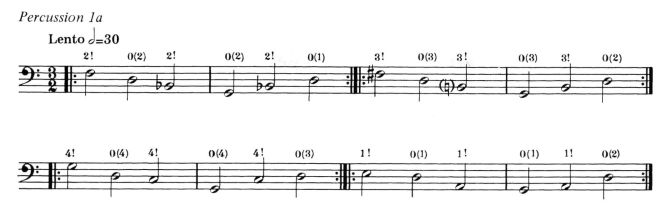

*Ex. 2*

Make sure you do it really slowly – this is the basic left-hand work, the benefits of which will flow into all your playing if done in a tranquil way. The '!' denotes the percussive strike, and the number in the brackets indicates the finger with which to pluck the open string. This left-hand pizzicato marks the beginning of the upward, tensing movement.

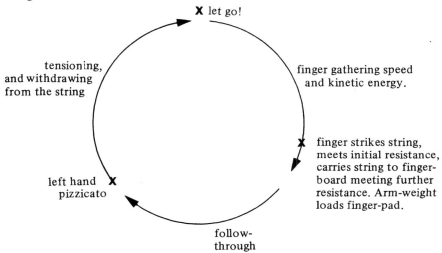

Each finger will be at a different stage in the cycle when we play if we can learn to tense just one finger at a time. Ideally each of the four fingers will flex thus:

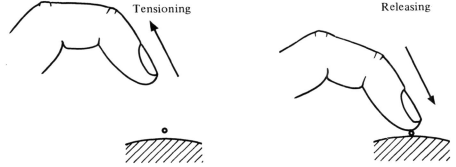

I am aware that to insist on this at the outset would be tautologous, but if you help matters out a little by a throw of the hand, please be aware of it and remember to remove this crutch when the fingers are stronger and the action is better. Note that the path of the distal phalanx is almost a straight line.

I am of course speaking of the development of finger action – independent of the hand and, later, independent of the other fingers – a prime prerequisite of virtuosity. Naturally when there is time, a throw of the hand to reinforce the finger-action, but not to supplant it, is not only permissible but desirable, bearing in mind the artistic situation. Furthermore these single 'hand-throws' will, in a slow phrase, be blended 'choreographically' into a smooth action, suggestive of and lending expression to the flow of the music (see p. 138).

Forgive me for labouring the point. In these days when we are driven not so much 'out-of-our-minds' as 'out-of-our-bodies', few people can dispose a clear attention to the functioning of the limbs from the 'inside', so to say.

The point is crucial, for we have before us an awful warning from the recent history of piano-playing. The valuable insights of Tobias Matthay were distorted by well-meaning followers so that finger training was neglected. Musical values became unbalanced consequent upon unbalanced body-use, and in many cases continual malfunction brought about such identifiable diseases as lordosis.

I might almost be persuaded to say that 'relaxation' is a dangerous word! Certainly it should be kept out of reach of 'children', and brought out only on special occasions under strict supervision!

If you become tired of Percussion 1a you may shift to:

*Percussion 1b*

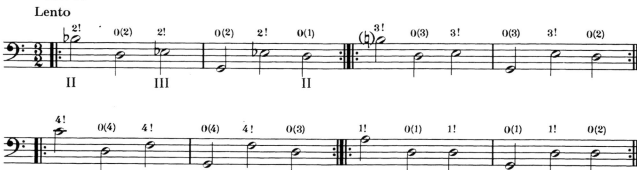

*Ex. 3*

and sometimes use other strings. It is certainly valuable to employ a few different rhythms:

lending more weight to the preparative phase of the cycle.

working on the deployment of arm-weight after the strike.

*Ex. 4*

and so on (see p. 11).

The only danger in these variants is that they may detract from the automatic habit of performing Percussion 1a daily for about two minutes. I would like you to build up an habitual regime of left-hand work that requires no conscious reinforcement, for it is the cumulative effect over the months and years that is valuable. Think of this work as a kind of technical hygiene like tooth-brushing.

It will have been seen that in the preceding work the finger is raised at least two inches (5 cm) from the string, slightly less, perhaps, with the third finger. Now, when we are playing, it is neither possible nor desirable in a rapid passage to raise the fingers so high, for any distance from the string has to be recovered, the round trip being accomplished in a fraction of a second. Thus it is important, having mastered the preceding activities, to forge a technique for clear enunciation in rapid passages; and here the principle of the uninvolved, quiet, hand becomes infrangible.

Maximum rise of finger: half an inch (1.25 cm).

Do not work these exercises when the hands are cold. Work towards equal loudness of the struck and plucked notes. Rest those fingers that are not working on the D string, thus:

*Percussion 2ax (L.H. alone)*
**Moderato**

also *Percussion 2ay*

Ex. 5

Later:

*Percussion 2bx*

*Percussion 2by*

9

*Percussion 2cx*

3!  1(3) 3!   4!  2(4) 4!

*Percussion 2cy*

1!   3! 1(3)   2!  4! 2(4)

*Percussion 2dx*   *2dy*

4!  1(4) 4!   1!  4! 1(4)

*Ex. 6*

## Percussion 2. Variants

These exercises may profitably be practised on other strings and in other positions. The height of the strings above the fingerboard at the 'neck' position (see p. 11 opposite) being greater, the need for clarity of left-hand finger-action becomes greater.

Having equated the loudness of the struck and plucked notes, occasionally work thus:

*f   p   f   p*
( also *p   f   p   f* )

*Ex. 7*

Notice that the dynamic pattern 'cuts-across' the strike/pluck pattern. This poses the need for even greater muscular discrimination: 'Ask, and it shall be given you.'

Other useful variants, spotlighting psychophysical inertia:

(i)

*f   p   f   p*
( also *p   f   p   f* )

(ii)

*f   p   f   p*      *f   p   f   p*
( also *f   p   f   p   f*      *p   f   p* )

*Ex. 8*

10

Add the original Percussion 2ax or another variant to the daily work.

There is a maxim amongst the farmers of the Dordogne – 'un peu de tout'. I'm sure this applies to technical practising. Small amounts of a wide variety of exercises bring us forward more rapidly to the point where the technique disappears and only the music remains.

Here is a useful exercise which gives more flexibility to the finger-joints, and hints at the all-important question of independence:

*Left hand*

*Ex. 9*

Use variously the fingerings (throughout the exercise):

      1234, 4321, 1324, and 4231.

Also:  1212, 2323, 3434,

      2121, 3232, and 4343

and invent further patterns.

Apply the above fingerings to:

*Ex. 10*

and occasionally work the whole exercise in the neck position. (The position defined by first finger placed on the equivalent stopped notes to the open strings.)

*Ex. 11*

When crossing the four strings, allow the left elbow to rise and fall naturally, but do not raise the shoulder. One must cultivate an 'interested' elbow, one that follows the activities of the left hand and gives support.

# Shifting (preliminary)

This is important in many ways, notably in intonation-control and in the initiation of the larger portamento-slides and the close control of smaller ones. It is sometimes objected that these things are best left to artistic feeling and that the necessary muscular control will arise naturally. It is my strong belief and experience that the more these matters are studied 'in vitro', so to say, the freer may be the emotion expressed. It is important to furnish the playing with a strong sense of technical *predictability*. This gives confidence and in turn initiates a beneficent spiral.

The following exercise, called 'Snakes' purely for simplicity of denotation, powerfully enlarges capability.

*Snakes (L.H. alone)*

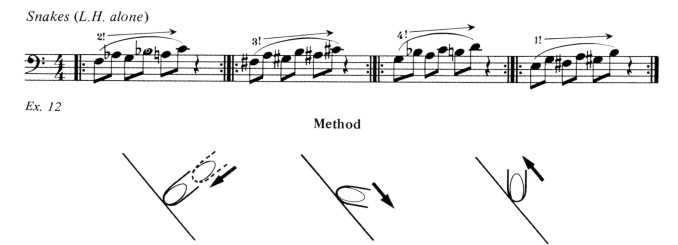

*Ex. 12*

**Method**

1 Strike the first note (F) percussively.
2 Keeping the finger-pad locked on to the note, incline the finger (and hand) as far bridgewards as possible.
3 Drag the pad along to the next note (A♭) with the hand. Keep the strongest contact with the string.
4 Drag the pad back to the third note, the finger now being inclined pegwards. Have a feeling that the pad is unwilling to budge, that it has to be dragged along, rather in the manner of the hairs of a large paintbrush charged with sticky paint. It should be possible to maintain the sound right through to the last note.
5 The thumb follows grudgingly, so to speak, thus exercising the hand muscles.
6 The forearm shares the torsional movement of the hand.

*Snakes, Variants:*

*Ex. 13*

Practise these also on the other strings.

## Mixed exercises

I think it is profitable now to combine some of the previous exercises in order to develop 'canniness' in the left hand. Hold the slid-to note until the percussion of the next note.

(*L.H. alone*)

*Ex. 14*

Hold the minim right through.

(*L.H. alone*)

*Ex. 15*

14

Occasionally vary the order of the plucking fingers, but keep that new order throughout the exercise.

A situation that arises constantly is that when one finger is being held, another must be struck or plucked. This 'bridging' requires that the held finger, from being a pivot, becomes one of the piers of a bridge, the other being the struck finger in the case of percussion. In the case of pizzicato the main hand-weight must be taken by the held finger. The importance of maintaining the balance of the hand in these circumstances, and of training the fingers to strike freely when one finger is shackled, cannot be overrated.

I will give you a piece of sugar. These exercises will greatly improve your Bach playing!

**Bridging exercises A\***

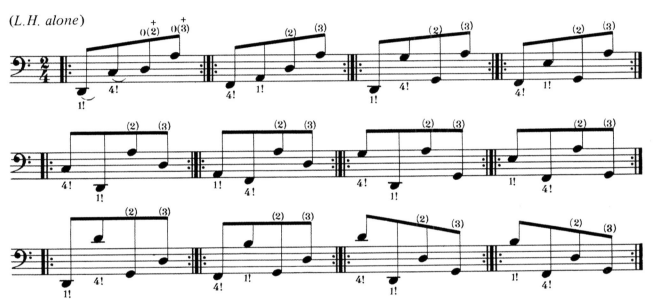

*Ex. 16*

The above may profitably be worked with the first two notes of each bar being played by 1 and 3, and plucked notes by 2 and 4. Work with circumspection, especially if you have a small hand.

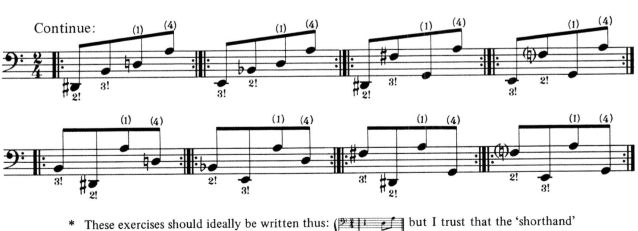

\* These exercises should ideally be written thus: but I trust that the 'shorthand' is understandable. Hold the first two notes through the bar.

This line should be attempted only after considerable training.

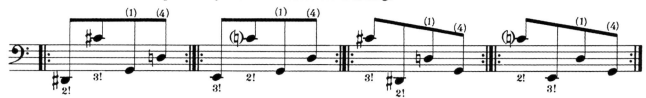

*Ex. 17*

*Ex. 18*

*Ex. 19*

*Ex. 20*

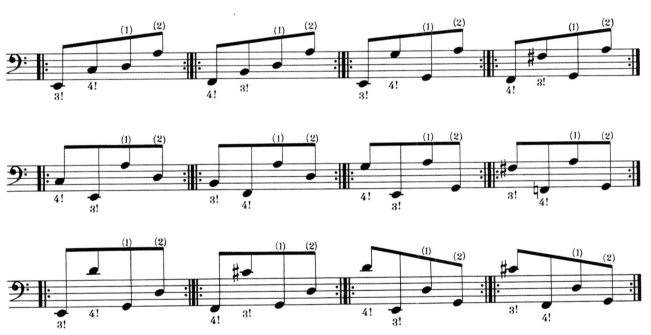

*Ex. 21*

This last exercise (21) bears especial attention, for it is commonly found that the third and fourth fingers are weak.

If some bars are found to be 'impossible', do not strain to achieve them, but put them on one side for later attention.

The repeat signs here are optional and each section may be worked as a continuous whole, but I counsel a rest before commencing the next section. Frequent short rests are essential.

I believe strongly in the interaction of the benefits accruing from a variety of exercises. After working these last examples I think you will perform better in Ex. 14, p. 13.

## Bridging exercises B*

1. A *little* vibrato will help to dissipate tension.
2. Release at the end of each bar.

*Ex. 22*

Occasionally reverse the striking order:

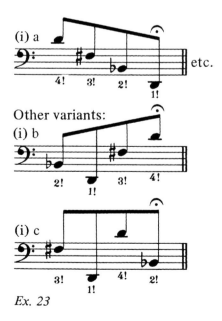

*Ex. 23*

---

\* These exercises should properly be written as below, but I trust the formula adopted is adequate. The fingers should be held down through the bar.

*Bridging*

Whereas a certain amount of muscular fatigue is inevitable and natural, one must heed the warning of pain. I have spoken of the advantage of rests; very short rests between smaller sections, longer rests after the larger divisions of material. However if there is pain one must cease work temporarily. The great piano pedagogue Leschetizky said that pain on the upper side of the forearm and hand is fairly acceptable but pain on the underside is very dangerous. From my experience this is true: one must just be sensible. I am sure it is of advantage to make a salad of finger-exercises and bowing exercises – 'un peu de tout'. Be careful in the latter part of the following exercise, especially if you have a small hand.

(ii) (extensions)

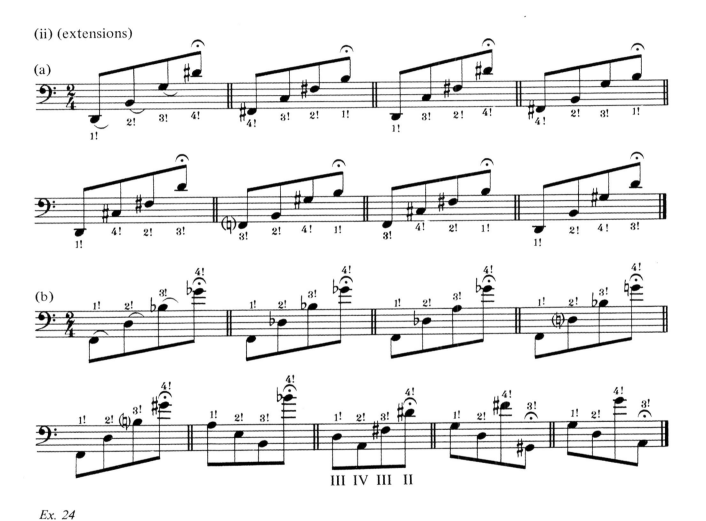

*Ex. 24*

Clearly, one may, as with the previous examples alter the striking order, and indeed invent many variants. This procedure should not be allowed to detract from the habit of following a certain schedule of work automatically. The cumulative effect over a period is what really produces results.

19

(iii) Fingers that must be re-positioned must not disturb the others.

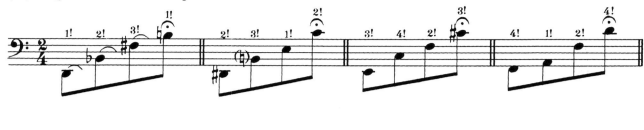

*Ex. 25*

(iv) a

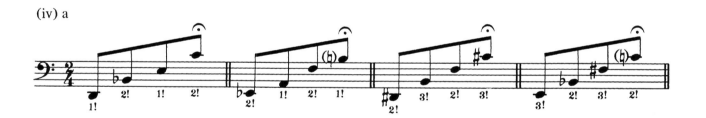

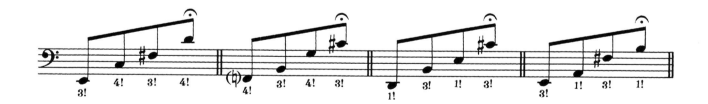

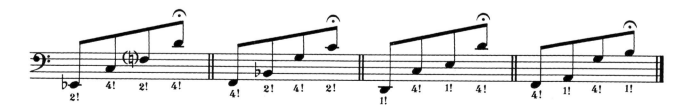

*Ex. 26*

(iv) b (alternative to (iv) a)

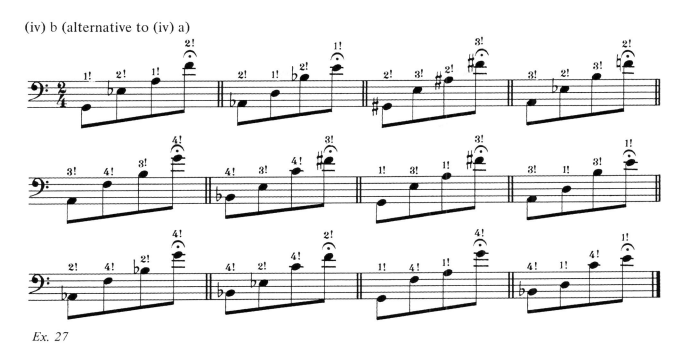

*Ex. 27*

As before, the foregoing may with advantage be practised with reversed and mixed striking orders.

I should perhaps utter some words of warning. *Any* change in one's playing arising from new procedures, even if it is wholly in a beneficial direction, is likely to upset the balance struck at any given time, and the playing may be disturbed as a result. It would be foolish to judge the procedures unsound upon this evidence. It would be even more foolish to embark for the first time upon this training within a few days of playing in public.

I have heard it said — by a pianist, but I can endorse it — that one should ease up slightly in the technical work just prior to public performance. One should 'coast' into it, so to speak. This is certainly true of intellectual work for an examination. I think the reason lurks in what I have said in the previous paragraph. One has to let things 'settle' a bit, to give scope to the integrative function. Certainly the audience must not be aware of the technique, but must feel that the music speaks to them directly — 'from the heart to the heart', as Beethoven said.

I must also warn, for much the same reasons, against expecting quick results. Many subtle readjustments have to take place in the nervous system before the new abilities become your property. There are all sorts of feedback questions to be resolved and also certain curious tautologies. For instance, until one feels confident in the predictability of the result one cannot be confident of the same predictability.

### Further training exercises for the left hand

(Practise the semiquaver exercises at first without the 'holding' fingers in place.)

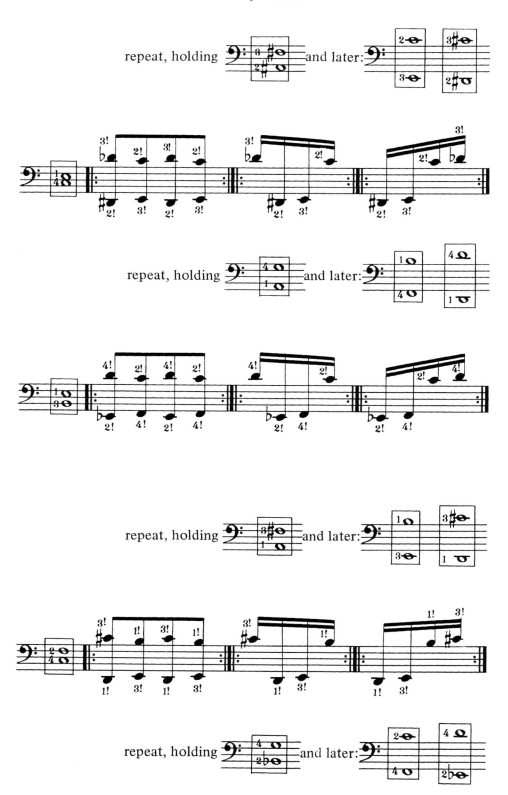

*Ex. 28*

* Do not worry that with the 'later' holding configurations not all the notes will actually sound.

# Pizzicato

As we have been dispensing with the bow for a while, perhaps we may continue thus and examine the question of pizzicato – a much neglected branch of technique. Of course, we must be able to perform pizzicato whilst still holding the bow, but it is nevertheless valuable to practise certain manoeuvres without it. (See plates 1 and 2 on p. 30 below.)

When time permits, by far the best sound is produced by using the thumb. Run the thumb down the side of the string, starting from about the region of the left-hand 'neck position', gathering speed until one reaches a spot near the end of the fingerboard. Here one makes a left-turn and continues the gesture in a curve until within a few inches of the left ear. With the A string there is no problem. With the lower three strings, naturally one must quit the string at a sufficient angle to avoid plucking the next higher string.

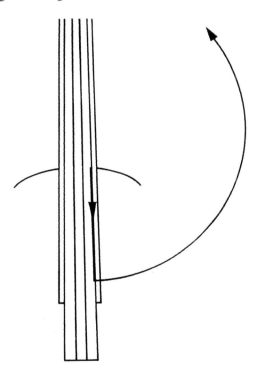

Why should one continue the gesture after the note has been played? As in tennis, it is the knowledge that one *intends* to follow-through that removes any inhibitions from the crucial moment.

Practise the following notes with vibrato. Find the note with minimum percussion, for otherwise a double note will be produced.

*Ex. 29*

Naturally the left-hand finger must be held down firmly to maintain the vibration for a long time.

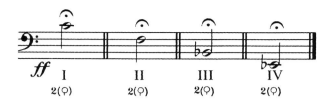

*Ex. 30*

I propose to adopt a terminology symmetrically congruent with those used for the left hand, though no codification has in fact been made. Thus ♀ = thumb, 1 = the index-finger and so on. (When the 'cellistic millennium dawns, the thumb will cease being a poor relation; piano-type finger-terminology, emancipated these many decades, will be adopted.)

Let us continue:

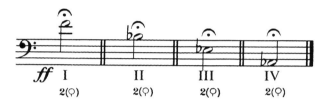

*Ex. 31*

It is important to be able to exclude the slightest sound during the rests, especially perhaps when playing for the microphone.

So far we have discussed what might be termed *pizzicato suono*. Very effective artistically is *pizzicato secco*.

One simply releases the pressure in the left-hand finger so that from being a 'bridge' it becomes a damper.

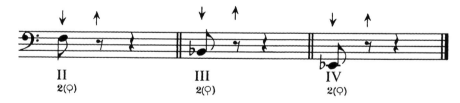

*Ex. 32*

Why have I omitted the C on the A string? Unless we damp the C string its second partial will become excited, thus ruining the *secco* effect. The damping can be done by another finger resting lightly on as dissonant a note as possible (removing the likelihood of cousinly excitation) – perhaps third finger on E would be best.

This damping problem arises frequently when an open string or a partial continues resonating even when the music has modulated into another key and the resonance becomes an embarrassment. When no finger is available for this work, I certainly do not rule out the use of the cheek! When the bow is not in use it is occasionally possible to employ the right hand, but then there is an attendant danger of getting a further sound on its removal.

So now we can add the C:

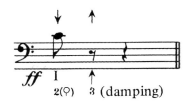

*Ex. 33*

One can run the gamut from the note allowed to resonate *a niente* to the completely *secco* sound.

We shall now limit the time interval but still employ the thumb. Make anticlockwise circles of about eight inches in diameter, flattening the tangent to a straight line against the side of the string of about three inches (76 mm) in length. Of course the first note may be prepared by a longer slide but this will give the note greater prominence.

*Ex. 34*

Practise it slowly at first.

Let us now take two strings. The procedure is much the same to begin with, but one crosses the lower of the two strings slightly at an angle. One comes to a momentary halt at the side of the upper string and then proceeds with plucking that one at right angles and then with the follow-through to the left ear.

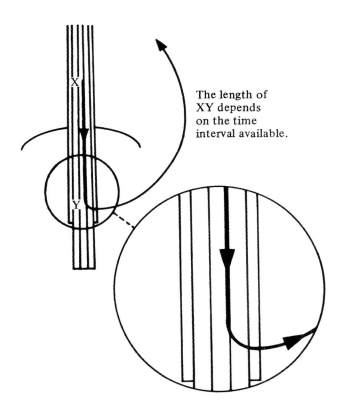

The length of XY depends on the time interval available.

25

Why do we only give the *upper* string the privilege of being plucked in the best way, viz. at right angles? The mass of the lower string is of necessity greater and, other things being equal, it can absorb and transmit greater energy. Thus, even to produce the subjective effect of *equal* loudness of the two notes one must adopt a procedure that will give preference to the string with the lesser mass. But musically one seldom wishes for equality, but rather that the top note should have a solo quality, the lower note suggesting a harmony. Thus the need for preferential treatment is doubly underlined. Practise the following in strict tempo. *Poco* vibrato. Make circles as before.

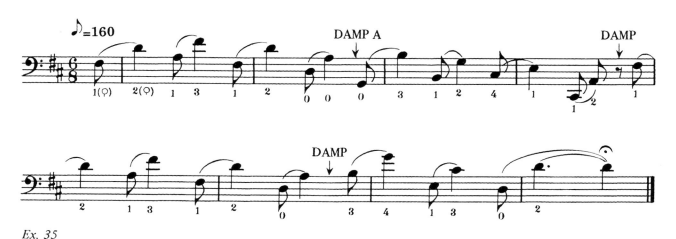

Ex. 35

In the second bar the damping is easily accomplished by the third finger near the first joint. In the fourth bar the hand as a whole can be used. Practise it slowly at first.

Let us now consider three strings. We make a paraboloid gesture giving the right-angle pluck only to the top string so that the melody may be enhanced. The pulse in this example is slower, so larger circles may be made. Metrical regularity is assured if there is a momentary pause with the thumb resting against the next string. Hold the chords through the bar. Do not strike the A string in the first three bars of the last line!*

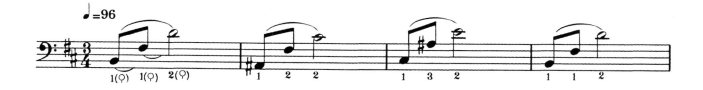

* In the Elgar concerto (second movement), in Henze's solo serenade (Tango movement), and in Britten's third solo suite (fifth movement, Dialogo), one plays three-note pizzicato chords in which the D string carries the melody, and the curving gesture of the right hand must then be taken upwards after that string has been played. It is advisable to stop the A string with any free finger, not wholly depressing the string (to provide a damping effect), and located upon a note which, if accidentally sounded, will at least be in a relevant harmony.

*Ex. 36*

Practise it slowly at first.

The same tactics apply when we take four strings:

*Ex. 37*

Practise it slowly at first. Don't forget that only the top string is plucked at right angles.

Occasionally one may need to make a rapid reiteration of chords such that there is not time for the anticlockwise movement with arm-participation described above. Adopting the general principle of limiting the number of limbs involved with increasing velocity we shall make a quick *clockwise* movement of the hand, a small sector of a circle, using a very flexible wrist. The last chord is played with an anticlockwise gesture.

*Ex. 38*

When performing this exercise holding the bow, one must adopt a loose hold, otherwise the motion will be transmitted to the stick, resulting in a diminution of the possible speed.

*Pizzicato secco* is easily accomplished here, simply by releasing the pressure of the left-hand fingers and using them as dampers:

*Ex. 39*

If the chord contains an open string, a free finger must damp that string, the rest being damped as above.

*Ex. 40*

The downward movement of the fourth finger must be coordinated with the upward release of the others.

When it is impossible to use the thumb for pizzicato, some approximation to its advantages may be made by 'binding' the first and second fingers together to make one big fat 'finger'.

It is useful to place the thumb on the edge of the fingerboard to the right of the C string. This acts as a pivot and helps to prevent accidents. Always pluck the strings near to the end of the fingerboard, unless there is some artistic reason to the contrary.

Many 'cellists only recognize a first-finger pizzicato. It is frequently adequate, but when the tempo exceeds a certain point, difficulties arise, or, in an extended passage, fatigue. Examples of the former can be found in Shostakovich's sonata and of the latter in Beethoven's 'Archduke' trio.

It might be valuable to see how fast one can play a scale pizzicato using only the first finger (with the thumb placed as suggested above. *Without* the thumb so placed the speed will be even further reduced).

Thus I suggest one should cultivate a technique using alternately first and second fingers.

*Ex. 41*

28

There is a certain symmetry here — the open strings are always plucked by the second finger. It would be misleading to suggest that this is always possible. It would be wise to take many passages and write in the pizzicato fingering you mean to adopt: do not leave it to chance.

*A short pizzicato study using first and second fingers*: keep the thumb on the side of the fingerboard, except for the last chord.

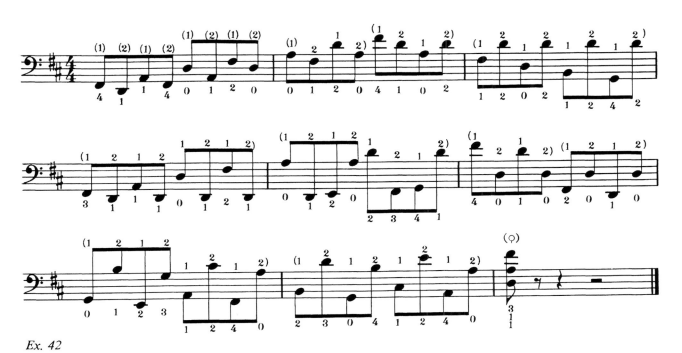

*Ex. 42*

This alternation provides the possibility of a fast tempo, but when practising it slowly for various reasons one may find two consecutive 1s or 2s more comfortable. Resist the temptation and acquire the (1,2) technique. One could of course finger the above (2,1) throughout, but I want to stress that you must arrange what you are going to do in a passage of music and stick to it.

All the foregoing can be easily performed whilst still holding the bow.

There are sometimes occasions when the problem is neatly solved by introducing a left-hand pizzicato, especially, but not necessarily, on open strings. (The sign for left-hand pizzicato is +.) Thus, in the study above, we can play:

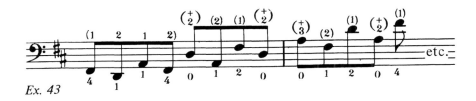

*Ex. 43*

Another example:

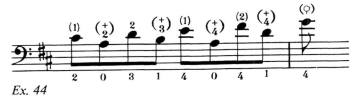

*Ex. 44*

29

You will note that the basic 1,2 pattern of the right hand is preserved, the left-hand pizzicati being substituted for whatever finger world normally have played the note.

We have considered chord-playing employing the thumb. This implies an *arpeggiando* effect. Sometimes we want the notes to sound together, so, as in a harpsichord, we use two or three fingers of the right hand as 'jacks', plucking upwards. It is here that some people object that they will drop the bow. Hold the bow as shown in the plates below and all will be well.

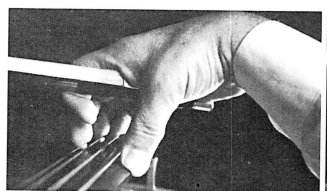 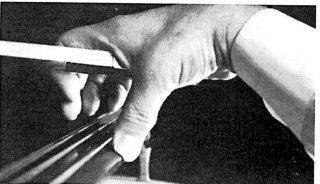

Pizzicato fingering throughout: (2,3,4)  ♀ placed on side of fingerboard as pivot.

'Harpsichord' pizzicato

Ex. 45

Clearly one can play any two strings with any two of the right-hand fingers:

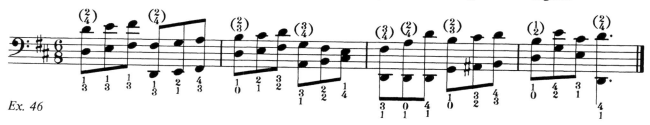

Ex. 46

However, in the case of pizzicato of the two outer strings, and this certainly occurs in modern works, one can get more sound by taking the C string with the thumb and the A string with 1 and 2 'bound-together' thus:

Ex. 47

* This chord could be fingered $\begin{smallmatrix}0\\3\\1\end{smallmatrix}$ but one must be careful not to touch the D string with (2).

30

I have mentioned modern music. One frequently has to be prepared to save composers from the consequences of their poverty of craftsmanship, the overt expression of their poverty of imagination. Often an 'arco' passage will lead straight into a pizzicato one, and vice versa. Appearances can usually be saved by judicious use of left-hand pizzicato, but what of:

*Ex. 48*

which is a translation of an actual example?

Here the solution is to extend the right-hand first or second finger and continue the bow-stroke trailing the fingernail across the strings, care being taken to pizzicato over the fingerboard, as rosin on the finger is unpleasant, upsets the control of the bow, and, with later pizzicati spreading it around the 'cello, ruins portamenti.

Whether it is, in the broadest sense, moral to cover up for unprofessional composers, is a question that must be left to the individual conscience. Be warned, however, not to expect any credit, for if matters go smoothly the critics will declare the music to have been superbly laid out for the instrument!

One frequently encounters rapidly reiterated chords, guitar-style, in Spanish and Italian music, and pastiches thereof.

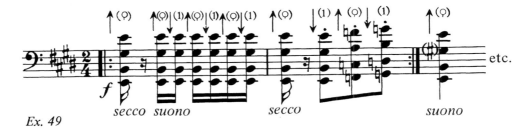

*Ex. 49*

Clearly the full preparation and follow-through is impossible. A quick flutter across the strings, backed up with vigorous arm action, and, for smoothness, preferably in an elliptical path:

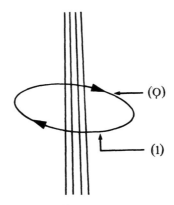

31

The following study combines all the modes of pizzicato we have been discussing.

## Pizzicato study

*Ex. 50*

∗ In this study I have slipped in a device without warning, but it is quite simple. The B is played by a strong percussion of the first finger of the left hand. The resonance is derived from a combination of the percussion and the residue of energy already in the string from the preceding pizzicato.

*Ex. 51*

When an open string is plucked and then stopped at a certain point, if one wishes for an equal apparent loudness there is a correlation between the delay before the second note and the pitch of that note, such that the greater the delay the higher must be the pitch of that note. This is because it takes less energy to give the same apparent loudness in a shorter length of string. Thus, while

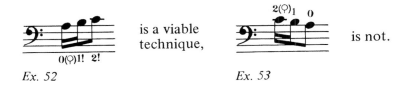

is a viable technique,

is not.

*Ex. 52*                            *Ex. 53*

However, we are still unbeaten, and indeed, unbowed! When we ascend we employ percussion, when we descend we employ a left-hand pizzicato.

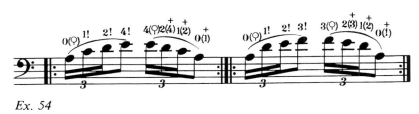

*Ex. 54*

# Articulation Exercises

Here is an exercise that stands midway between exercises for the finger considered in isolation, and those designed to promote that all-important factor, independence, and is performed with the bow.

Set the metronome to 100 and count eight ticks per note per bow-stroke. Work the exercise in two ways: (i) increasing the rising distance and tension throughout the eight beats, releasing finally on to the note at the denoted moment, springing up again immediately, (ii) 'pulling-out' the finger four times, increasingly far and tense, on the first, third, fifth and seventh beats, with an extra little one on top (added to whatever has been achieved on the seventh) on the eighth beat. Of course the bow must go along utterly unconcerned with the gymnastics of the left-hand fingers. Sometimes bow '*f*', sometimes '*p*'. Above all, no jerks at the changes. Rest the fingers that are not working on their respective places in the first position. The working finger must naturally conform to the finger-action patterns shown on page 7 above.

(a) HOLD

\* A slight left-hand pizzicato helps the string to 'speak' promptly.

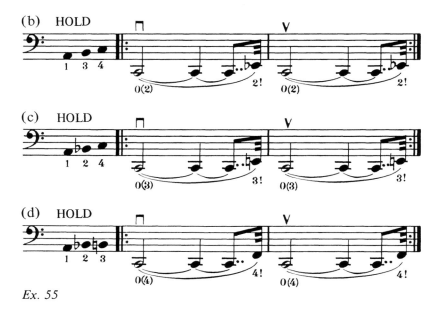

*Ex. 55*

Now reverse the finger-action. On ♪ the finger must rise as high as possible. As before, adopt two ways: (i) allowing the left arm-weight to flow increasingly as the eight beats progress, (ii) pressing down into the string on the first, third, fifth and seventh beats. See if all this can proceed without an increase of tonus in the resting fingers – no easy task! Make sure that pressure changes in the left finger-pads have no correlation in the bowing. (Compare Stutschewsky, *Studien zu einer neuen Spieltechnik*, Schott edn 1371, modern edn, vol. 1, p. 8.)

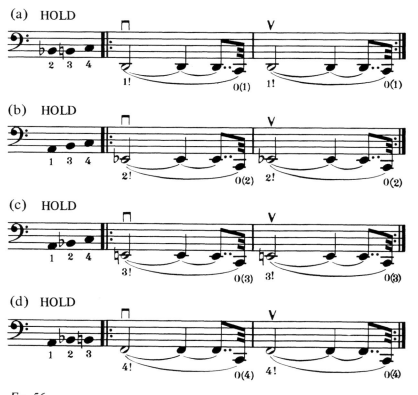

*Ex. 56*

*Ex. 57*

Occasionally work the foregoing, Exx. 55-7, raising the working finger only slightly above the string.

In order to make Exx. 55-7 more cogent after, one must insist, some months of working them in their 'natural' state, substitute in 55 and 56 the following 'holds' on the D string, the working finger still playing on the C string:

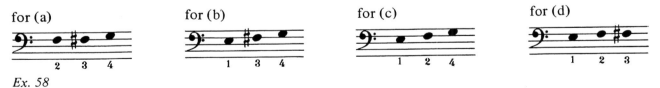

*Ex. 58*

in 57 substituting:

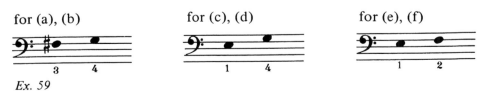

*Ex. 59*

Also, using the original 'holds' substitute the following for the working finger:

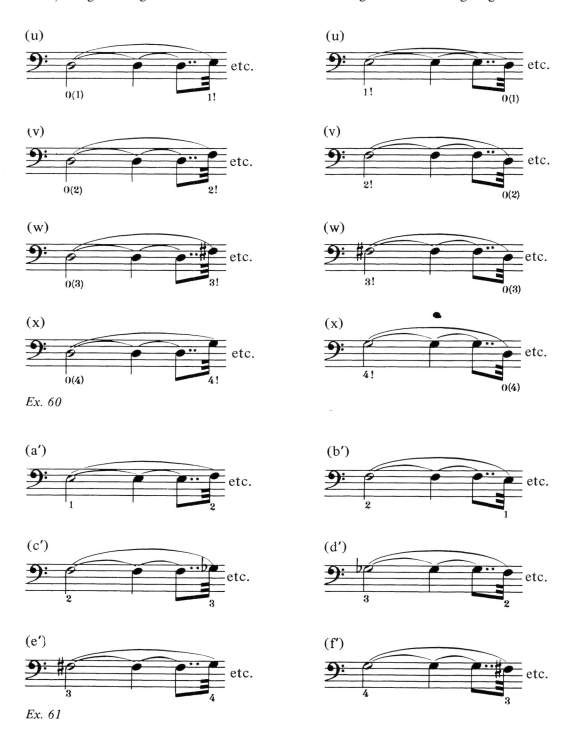

*Ex. 60*

*Ex. 61*

Then to make the exercise more cogent after a while substitute the following 'holds':

for (a')(b')     for (c')(d')     for (e')(f')

*Ex. 62*

And so, after all this time, we have arrived at the secret of clear 'cello-playing, at least from the left-hand point-of-view. If all players would allow the fingers to fall with the kinetic touch in ascending motifs, and pluck the strings slightly in descending ones, there would be an end to the wool-spinning that one so frequently hears. I rush to add that all this must be done with intelligence, and related to the artistic situation.

It is worth saying that when one is playing pianissimo the question of left-hand clarity assumes even greater importance, but a high percussion and violent plucking will destroy the mood. So, by practising Percussion 2 (p. 10 above), where the fingers do not rise very high, one can attack the strings clearly without objectionable bangings. This exercise is also vital to the question of sheer velocity. The rôle of the bow in promoting clarity of utterance is described in volume 1 of this essay.

# Phase 2.
# Finger Independence

If you have been performing the exercises regularly whilst reading this book there will surely be more craft in the fingers – a greater flexibility, and the mental cunning to use it to good effect.

Indeed, we are almost ready to make a start! First, however, we must consider the all-important question of finger independence. I cannot stress too strongly the vital nature of this quality. I am prepared to assert that fine 'cellists have finger independence invariably, and incompetent 'cellists have no finger independence, also invariably!

If the training of the finger itself might be called Phase I, then we can denote the training of the fingers to work independently and sequentially, as Phase 2.

By 'sequentially' I mean that each finger must be found at any moment to be at the right point in its cycle of operations. Thus, whilst one finger may be striking the string (releasing), another may be just starting its up-stroke (tensioning). This clearly demands close attention until it becomes automatic. We must assume that all the mental and physical prerequisites for differentiation-of-function are present (see Prelude).

My experience is that most 'cellists with a little thought and work can quickly establish a good functioning of fingers 1, 2, and 3. Many have difficulty, however, with the fourth finger, and thus we have to consider this problem separately.

The bugbear is again our ancient enemy — compensation. The 'cellist with the weak, untrained, possibly very short, little finger often stiffens it up, and also the side of the hand to which it is attached, and then belabours the string with this composite and insensitive gadget. The hand then resembles a racehorse with one leg smitten by laminitis. Independent functioning is ruled out, velocity is excluded, and vibrato on the fourth finger – often the *most important* finger, as it plays the melodic-summit note – becomes the querulous shaking of a wooden crutch.

I do hope I have frightened you! But there is worse to come! It is very difficult to have one part of the hand in spasm and the rest free. This locking tends to spread to the rest of the hand with results that surely need not be spelled out.

I do not underestimate the courage needed to sort this out. *Il faut reculer pour mieux sauter*, and one may well have to experience the humiliation of playing much worse with the fourth finger and of experiencing its true weakness before things may march forward again.

Everybody has their own mode of habit breaking. For this player the best method will be to say 'from this moment I will not use my fourth finger unless correctly'; for that one, the professional player perhaps, 'I have to play constantly and cannot disturb the status quo overmuch, but I will devote ten minutes a day to this and hope that gradually it will percolate through into all my playing.' The player with a locked hand due to faulty use of the fourth finger can but dimly imagine the delight of a free hand. Expressiveness is liberated, and difficult passages become easy. When we remind ourselves that it is the *acceleration* of the finger as it hits the string, and not strength, that brings clarity, we can be confident that the 'little' finger can play as effectively as its bigger brothers.

I see no reason why the 'cellist should not cultivate that equality of touch that is the *sine qua non* of piano playing.

*Exercise for the fourth finger – remember!*

*Ex. 63*

38

And, with lateral movement:

Only once per day please. This is a very potent exercise: do please be circumspect.

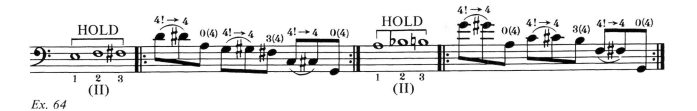

*Ex. 64*

I have no wish to duplicate the inspired contributions to left-hand independence made by others and would like to draw your attention to three fine sets of exercises.

The first pages of Cossmann's *Studien* (Schott edn 964) are excellent in their fiendish exposure of weakness and should be part of the basic technical diet. Stutschewsky, in his *Studien zu einer neuen Spieltechnik* (Schott edn 1371, modern edn., vol. 1, p. 50, section E), adds the open string to the yoke, thus raising the question of the pivoting and balance of the hand. Benedetti, in his *24 exercices en doubles notes* (Delrieu, Nice, 1955) takes the hand through all the positions thus adding a wonderful flexibility and intonation-control capability. His exercises also raise the question of intonation compromise as between the demands of harmony and those of counterpoint (see Creative Intonation).

I find that players who pursue extended work on these exercises develop rapidly an independence of the fingers and flexibility of the hand that would be difficult to duplicate by another course.

However, I would like to add another idea for which I am indebted to the late Alfred Cortot. In his *Principes Rationnels*, he has one finger held, whilst the others exercise, and calls it *le doigt témoin*. Brahms, in his fifty-one studies for the piano, uses substantially the same principle. I find that having one note held, and, in short, ignored, with the constant muscle-tonus implied, and then exercising with the constantly varying muscle-tonus of the other fingers, one gains an extraordinary facility and insight into 'lightness' and 'heaviness' of the fingers. Moreover, this forms a good springboard for velocity exercises and the necessary reduction of note-pattern preferences.

Shake the left hand after each group: this will dissipate any residual tensions.

Raise each finger after use, rather in the manner of piano-playing. Sometimes put four or six four-note groups in each bow.

*With the bow:*                    sometimes $f$, sometimes $p$

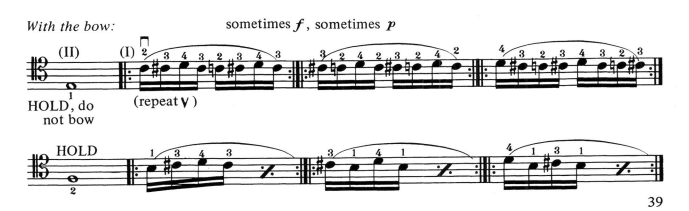

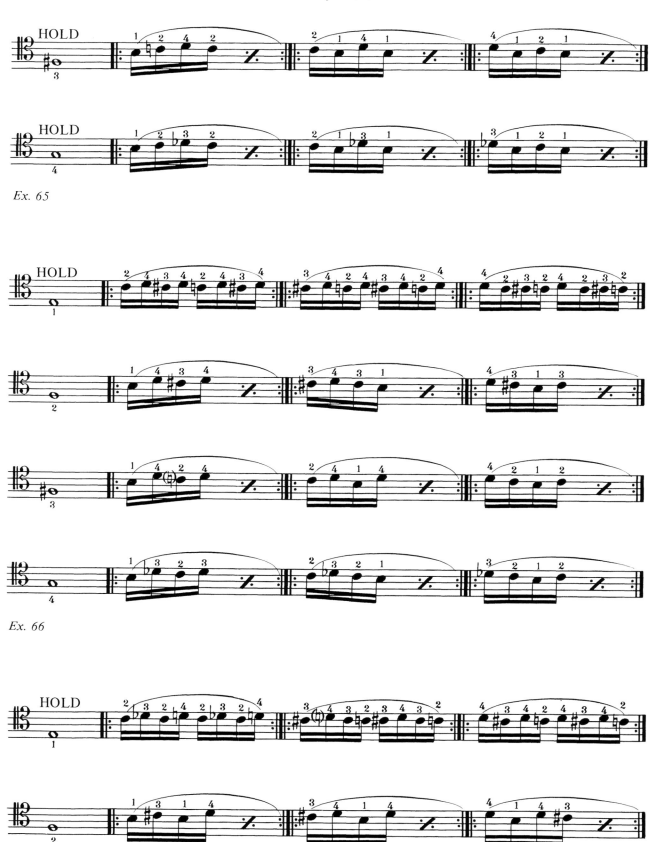

Ex. 65

Ex. 66

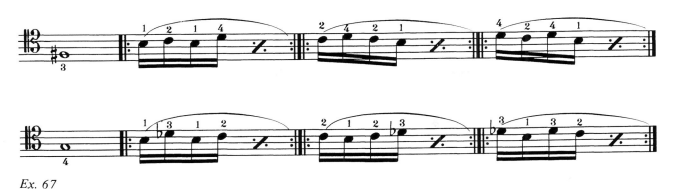

*Ex. 67*

Occasionally put the holding fingers on the G string thus:

*Ex. 68*

When time is limited, one may adopt the following formula:

*Ex. 69*

I think it is also valuable to work these exercises in the 'neck-position' see p.
As before, work them sometimes *f*, sometimes *p*. Occasionally put the 'witnessing' fingers on the G string thus:

*Ex. 70*

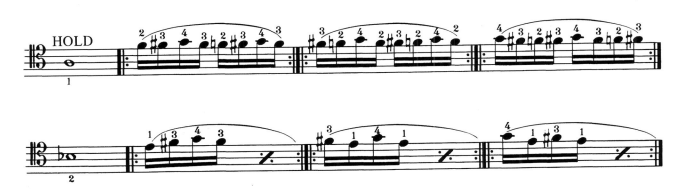

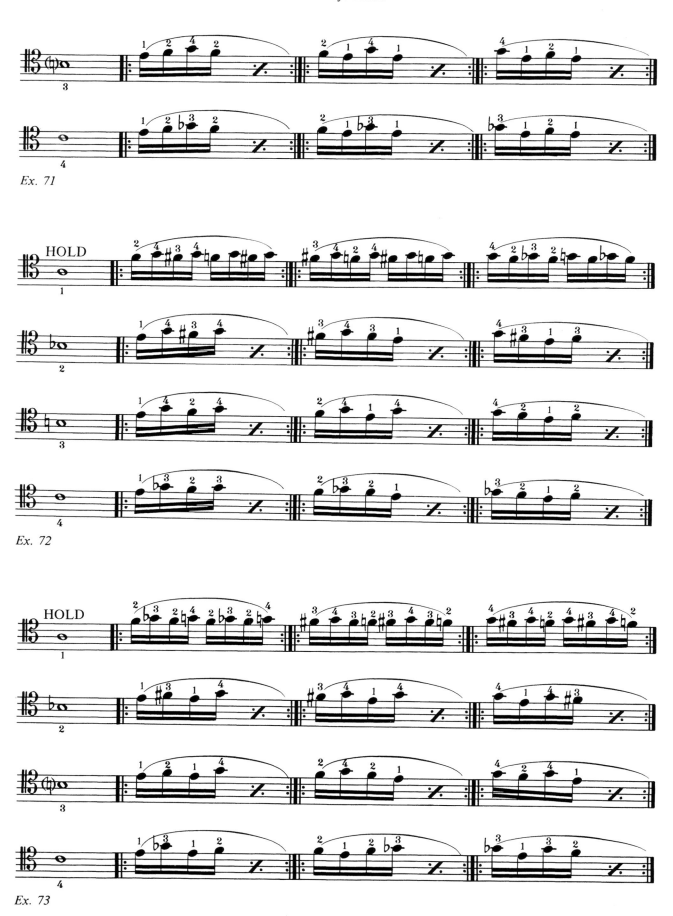

*Ex. 71*

*Ex. 72*

*Ex. 73*

## Finger Independence

We may extend this idea to embrace the ♀-positions. It is convenient to have the following exercises here, though ideally they would not be attempted before mastering the section on the ♀-positions as they require more flexibility than do the preceding examples. Keep your fingernails fairly short!

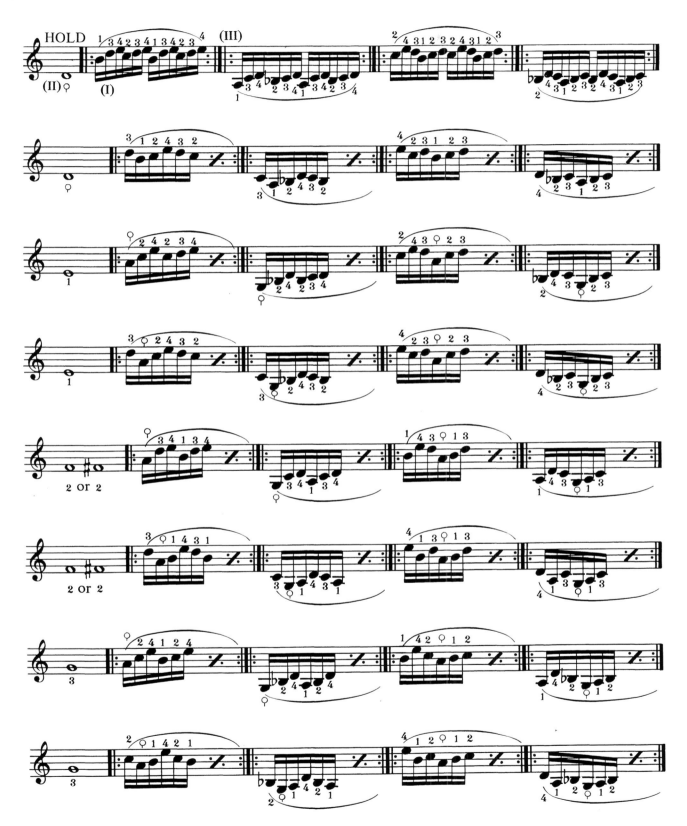

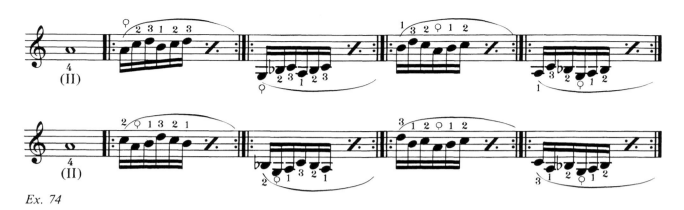

*Ex. 74*

If you are still 'web-handed' after all this, here are some more exercises that ought to help you. Hold the dotted minim throughout the bar, but do not sound it. Aim to achieve a legato running continuously throughout the six bars.

**Moderato, legato**

*Ex. 75*

and then repeat with the bars played in reverse order.

*Ex. 76*

as before repeat with the bars played in reverse order.

*Ex. 77*

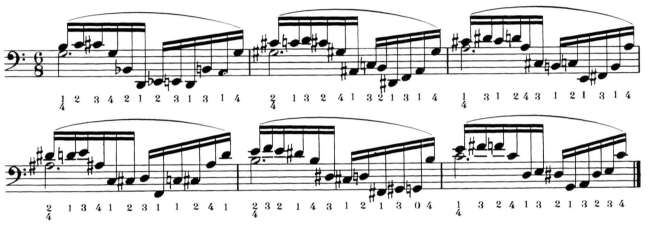

*Ex. 78*

Hold the dotted minim but do not bow it.

**Scherzando**

*Ex. 79*

*Ex. 80*

*Ex. 81*

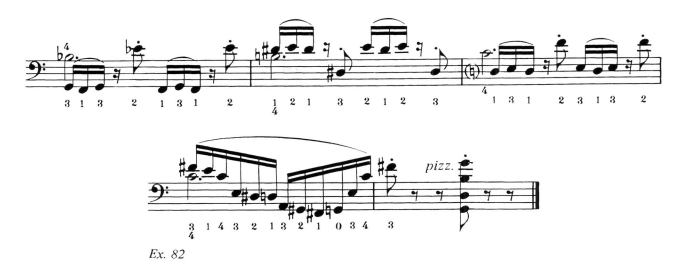

*Ex. 82*

# The Vibrato

It is with a measure of diffidence that I approach the subject of the vibrato. It arouses violent passions amongst the adherents of this or that 'cellistic sect. Perhaps this is understandable because it is so intimately bound up with personal artistry. I often think that the various and opposing theories that are canvassed so vehemently are really rationalizations of personal preferences, and maybe I too will be accused of just this failing! However I will rush in while the angels are still arguing.

Firstly, what the vibrato should *not* be. It should not be an all-purpose varnish laid on thickly over a bad painting to conceal its defects. It is not the side-show barker 'crying-up' his wares to catch the undiscriminating, knowing that his wares are essentially shoddy.

Unfortunately there is nowadays an hysterical pseudo-intensity concealing an inner deadness, a lack of the real drama, of arsis and thesis, of the incarnation of feelings and forms. The vibrato is often pressed into the service of this hysteria.

Vibrato is more properly an integral part of the sound and of the expression. It is personal and it is sincere. When I say 'sincere' I naturally exclude the 'sincerity' of the well-intentioned (see Stanislavsky!). I am speaking of the *conscious* sincerity of the true artist.

I feel that it is useful to make a distinction between the vibrato inherent in the beauty of sound, and the more exotic vibratos suitable for specialized expressive requirements. Sometimes a student will see a master-'cellist perform a bizarre vibrato, and because it is exactly right for some specific expressive idea, he will copy it in *all* his playing, with disastrous results.

What we need therefore is a basic vibrato that will enhance the sound, and then move on from there. Thus, with your indulgence, we will make an excursion into geometry.

Consider the motion of a point on the circumference of a circle such that it moves at a constant speed. It has a constant angular velocity, that is to say, in equal amounts of time (t) covers equal angular displacements ($\theta$).

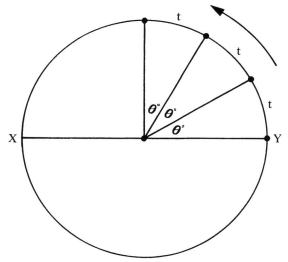

Now we are going to drop perpendiculars from the moving spot on to the diameter line.

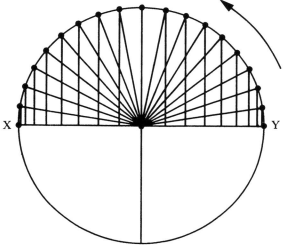

and as the spot continues around to where it started, Y, we send up perpendiculars again to the diameter, so the complete picture is:

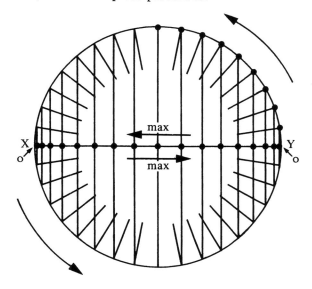

Now consider the motion along the diameter of the spot at the foot of the perpendicular. It is quite different from that of the spot moving around the circumference with constant angular velocity. It starts at Y with zero velocity. Then it moves leftwards towards the centre, increasing in speed all the time, until, just as it goes through the centre, it is momentarily going as fast as the spot on the circumference. Then, continuing to the left, it slows up progressively until it gets to X when, of course, its velocity is again zero. Then, continuing the cycle, it journeys from X back to Y, at first accelerating to a maximum in the centre of the circle, and then decelerating to zero at Y.

Now this motion along XY is called Simple Harmonic Motion and is the basis of all sound waves. Let us take XY and stand it on end and draw a line through the centre. This line will represent time.

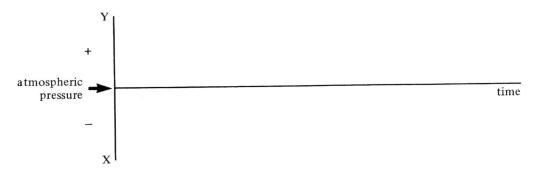

The plus and minus signs represent merely a mathematical polarity; no denigration of the activities below the line is intended! Now if we add to the Simple Harmonic Motion the dimension of time we get a sine wave, and this represents graphically the pattern of pressures (+) and vacuums (−) inherent in the act of hearing a pure note.

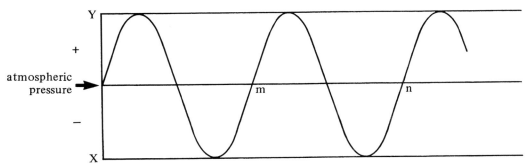

The cycle completes itself at m and n. The frequency is the number of times the cycle takes place every second. In the case of the open A string this cycle happens 221 times in a second.

Without wading into the marshy bogs of aesthetic theory I think we can say fairly confidently that one of the prime and recognizable components of Beauty, and, indeed, Truth!, is simplicity. Most races and tribes appear to recognize Pythagoras' demonstration of the two-to-one ratio of the octave, and also the three-to-two ratio of the fifth.

I am fully aware that another component of beauty is a 'humanizing' and 'imperfecting' of the platonic. Indeed, the emotional response may arise precisely by reason of the poignant tension between the ideal, or the idealized, and what is realizable. Nevertheless, I believe that our basic vibrato must be in Simple Harmonic Motion.

Thus, we take our XY axis, bend it a little, and use it to describe the motion of any point on the finger.

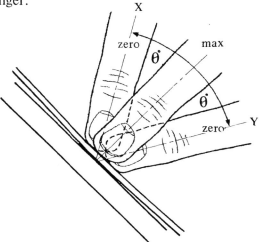

Naturally I have had to simplify matters somewhat. I have assumed that all the fingers are the same. I have ignored, for the moment, the thumb. I do not deal with the longitudinal waves set up in the string as a result of the vibrato.

Nevertheless, I think I illustrate certain cardinal points. As the finger rolls bridgewards the pitch is, of geometrical necessity, slightly sharpened. On rolling pegwards the pitch is correspondingly flattened. It is my contention that for the basic vibrato this sharpening and flattening, and the associated angles of displacement, should be equal, for the aesthetic reason cited above. That is to say that the motion should be symmetrical for reasons of simplicity.

Now we must take a broader view of the situation. Let us shift our viewpoint through 90 degrees.

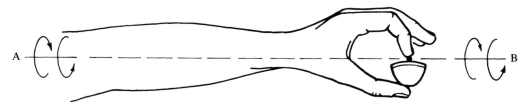

The arm and the hand must vibrate torsionally *as one unit* about the axis AB. Any flexion, or raising and lowering, of the wrist will complicate the movement and vitiate the effect. Quite apart from the geometrical considerations, flexion of the wrist means that we lose the mass of the forearm in its rôle as an oscillating fly-wheel. In the case of the violin this forearm rôle is undesirable, unnecessary, and, indeed, impossible! But then the violinist does not have to bring into play the magnitude of the forces commensurate with the massive strings, wood masses and air volumes of the 'cello.

Now, however persuaded you may be by the theory, you may say: 'How on earth can I reproduce this Simple Harmonic Motion?' Fortunately the mechanical properties of the forearm can be made to approximate to those of a torsional spring. Perhaps you have seen those mantelpiece clocks that have a massive horizontal flywheel hanging on a torsional spring. This regulates the required periodicity.

Thus, if we start with the finger upright (at right angles to the string) and angle it over bridgewards, we require something to slow things up progressively until at the moment of maximum deflection the movement is zero. Now in a torsional spring — and the forearm can approximate to this — the restoring force, i.e. the force tending to restore matters to the *status quo ante*, is proportional to the deflection. So, all we have to do is to arrange matters such that the restoring force exactly counterbalances the deflecting force at the moment of maximum deflection. Once the action is under way, of course, momentum has the greatest say.

So far it is plain sailing, *n'est-ce-pas*? There is one trifling difficulty that need not detain us long. We have agreed, I trust, that it is desirable that the angle of deflection bridgeward should equal the angle of deflection pegward. Unfortunately it is my experience that many people are disinclined, if you will forgive the pun, to do this, either from physical stiffness or from a faulty notion of what is involved.

However one can easily train oneself to get this equiangular movement. Rigorous application to the exercises called 'Snakes' (p. 12 above) will give the required plasticity, though, of course, in the case of the vibrato the finger-pad stays firmly on the same place — subject to the rolling action previously described.

Actually this might be the moment to inveigh against that most abominable of vibratos, where the finger-pad moves to and fro along the string.* If your artistic standards lie in the shady abysses inhabited by the more hysterical coloratura sopranos, then we part company right here! Fortunately it is not my business to teach people how not to play the 'cello so no more ink need be wasted.

I think I have described clearly the desiderata for a natural vibrato related to one finger. The upper arm is uninvolved except for a fleshy wobble in the more corpulent.

There is no problem with the vibrato of the thumb. The same free action already described serves us well. Naturally the symmetry of oscillation is more difficult to maintain, and I think one would ideally plan to avoid the thumb on a longish expressive note. However two examples spring to mind where we are forced to use the thumb expressively: (i) the beginning of the short C major section of the slow movement of Haydn's D major concerto and (ii) the two occasions in his C major concerto's slow movement where double-stopping forces a lyrical use of the thumb.

Now we must think about what happens when we play a group of notes. We have worked carefully to acquire the natural kinetic touch. We have worked to acquire independence of the fingers, keeping the hand as a still platform.

The next stage in our vibrato study must be to take these qualities and integrate them in a flowing choreography of fingers, hand and forearm. It is a hard step for the novice. It is equally hard for the developed player to remember what the difficulty once was. In this it is perhaps akin to the steps in learning to drive. At first one cannot imagine how one will ever coordinate meaningfully the necessary actions of the hands and feet, but after a while the organizational hierarchies establish themselves harmoniously.

What appears to happen when things are going well is that the last oscillation of the first note of the group is completed during the beginning of the second note, the new finger having struck kinetically just as the hand-forearm reached the half-way mark. The motion is thus uninterrupted and the weight transfer is completed smoothly. The kinetic falling action of the finger is reinforced by the rolling action of the hand.

I beg you to notice that this is *not* in conflict with my previous stricture about denying oneself hand movements when training the fingers to be independent. It

* I make an exception in the case of bar 12 of the second movement of Debussy's sonata.

is a question of different stages of development. Furthermore, in the case of revisionary technical practices this distinction must be clearly made and maintained.

So, now let us put all this into practice. I propose the following exercise as a beginning: without the bow, practise the equiangular movement already described, completing the cycle every $\frac{1}{100}$ of a minute, i.e. set the metronome to 100 and arrive at the bridgeward zero-point at every tick. If you use a strong percussion you can begin to hear the effect.

After a few unmetered passes try:

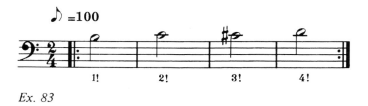

*Ex. 83*

As the finger strikes, go straightaway to the bridgeward zero-point (Y), and thereafter coordinate the ticks with Y.

If you do not want to introduce the complication of vibrato-transfer straightaway you could repeat the percussion four times on each successive finger thus:

*Ex. 84*

Repeat Ex. 82 with the bow, at first with one bow-stroke (not necessarily a full one) to a bar, later one bow-stroke to two bars. Now repeat with the metronome set at 120.

Before we proceed I must warn you that great patience is needed in delaying the advance to each successive stage, patience that will be rewarded. Bull-at-a-gate tactics will be self-defeating. Remember Alexander's 'Means Whereby' (volume 1, Prelude).

Now set the metronome to 144 and make eight wobbles, one per tick, on the semibreve (always counting from Y),

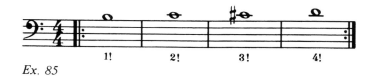

*Ex. 85*

without, and then with, the bow.

Now we are on the threshold of the natural torsional periodicity of the hand-forearm, and thus at the moment of the greatest temptation! (I've got it! I can dispense with the metronome!)

Put the metronome on 160, and continue work with Ex. 84 (one wobble per tick).

Now I want you to take a step *backwards* and to practise *two* wobbles per tick, the metronome being set at 60. Now this is slower than two wobbles per tick at 80 (the equivalent of one wobble at 160), which we have just achieved. *Reculez pour mieux sauter!*

Go for a *triplet* of wobbles on each crotchet tick at this speed (60). Work each finger severally.

Ex. 86

The reason I begin to organize the wobbles into groups of three is that one can thus achieve more frequent reiterations with a slower pulse than is possible with duple organization. If you wish to run down an escalator quickly, organize your steps into a compound metre!

Finally step up the metronome to 72.

Every player will reach the point at which he wants to discard the metronome at a different speed thereof. This is due to differences in inner looseness (a spiritual quality), and sheer mechanical considerations such as the bulk of the arm and hand, and the effect of this on the natural torsional periodicity. In general the rule is to stay 'in prison' as long as possible! Premature release is not beneficial.

After this work has been maintained for a while, practise free vibrato on one note, and then the following without, and later with, the bow.

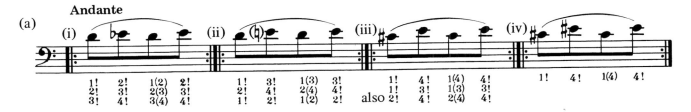

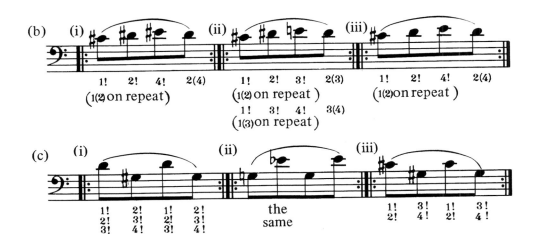

*Ex. 87*

The same continuity of the vibrato must be maintained through the shifts:

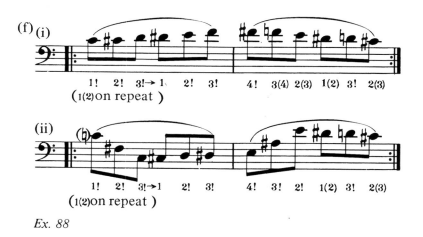

*Ex. 88*

These last two can clearly be worked together as a four-bar exercise.

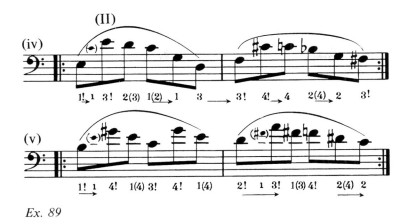

*Ex. 89*

I think it would be a good exercise to work the foregoing using two bars to a bow.

It will be noticed that some of the above examples may be played with a lazy use of the fingers, Ex. 86 (c) (i) for instance, to a lesser extent (c) (ii) and, still lesser (c) (iii), (d) (i) and (ii) and (e) (i) – (iv), that is to say that the fingers may be held down as a chord. Although this technique might have its place, it would clearly vitiate our efforts to establish an integration of the kinetic touch, the rolling hand-choreography and the vibrato-transfer.

There comes a speed of notes beyond which it is not possible to execute the vibrato. This speed is much faster than many players appear to think, and I recall the great violist Lionel Tertis' impassioned plea – 'keep the hand alive!' Remember also Eisenberg's 'The Living Hand'.

A cardinal point is that the weight of the hand-forearm must be concentrated upon the finger playing NOW. The NOW is all we really experience, the rest is memory or anticipation. If, instead of mentalizing the 'positions' as a sort of map-grid, you 'play' the positions, moving the hand from one fixed conformation to another, you will always be off-balance, the weight will be in the wrong place, and the vibrato ruined.

In such a case as ♯ some players would even hold the first finger down on the D whilst playing the F♯! Clearly a free, singing vibrato on the F♯ would then be impossible. Naturally I sympathize with the teachers of beginners and elementary players who tell their charges to adopt this practice when the geography of the 'cello is as yet a mystery, but it must be abandoned as soon as possible. Failure to take this vital step lies at the root of much stilted playing.

In general the hand should be fairly closed up, the fingers constellated around the playing finger. Clearly the moment-of-inertia is altered if the hand be opened. (Skating champions use this effect when they suddenly close their arms in, during a spin, thus, due to the conservation of angular momentum, greatly increasing the angular velocity.)

Thus the sort of action I am advocating is the antithesis of the aims of time-and-motion study! In the case just cited we remove the finger-clustering around the first (on the D) to a cluster around the fourth (around the F♯). I suppose that a time-and-motion study with mechanical efficiency as its sole criterion would dictate precisely that position-holding that rules out expressivity and flowing-hand choreography.

But, *per contra*, when we exceed that speed at which the vibrato is still possible, then the most economical and sure hand-placing is of the essence, and to move the hand in a smooth chain of 'shapes' becomes the best way of proceeding. Here of course there must be no clutching of the instrument, using the 'cello as a walking-stick, or thumb-locking. The shoulder joint must be free to permit the rapid shifts.

When we come to the question of the vibrato of chords, clearly the hand cannot have the same freedom that it enjoys with single notes. The larger the distance between the stopping fingers, the greater the constriction. Thus:

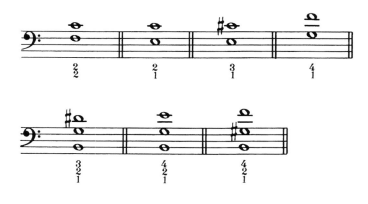

Compare:

*Ex. 90*

Whatever the case, the vibrato must be symmetrical about the mean position.

It always surprises me that the beautiful effect of the vibrated harmonic is so neglected. It can easily be executed whether on the true harmonic or on the artificial one, though naturally the latter suffers some of the drawbacks of the vibrated chord. Both the vibrated and the unvibrated harmonics in Shostakovich's first concerto can provide a perfect foil to the sounds of the celeste. There is, moreover, nothing to prevent us vibrating harmonic-chords or, indeed, chords composed of one stopped note and one harmonic.

Mention must be made of the vibrato of the open string. This can be accomplished in two ways. The first is simply to place the first finger on the top nut (where the strings pass over into the peg box) and vibrate. Here, of course, only the pegward half of the vibrato is effective, but at least it helps to avoid the dead sound of the open string, unless, of course, precisely this dead sound is, at some point, artistically suitable. Part of the effect of this vibrato is doubtless the movement of the whole 'cello and the effect this has on the bowing. Certainly I think that one should consider employing this technique in Fauré's *Elégie*.

The second way of effecting the vibrato of the open string is to vibrate an acoustically similar or related note, thus activating a vibrato in the open string by sympathetic vibration. Thus:

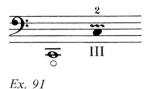

*Ex. 91*

Clearly it is easier for the lower strings, by reason of their greater mass, to influence the higher strings, than the converse.

So far we have been thinking about the basic vibrato, the regular undulations that give a singing quality. We must now consider some variations of this.

A broad rule — but with *so* many exceptions! — would be: 'the lower the note the wider and slower should the vibrato be, and, contrariwise, the higher the note, the faster and narrower'. Thus is maintained a sort of balance of the total energy, a factor that becomes paramount in the case of the syllabic diminuendo (see vol. 1, p. 90).

Fortunately, if the natural movement of the hand-forearm and upper-arm linkage be followed logically, and indeed geometrically, from first position to the topmost thumb-positions, the longitudinal component of the vibrato is reduced by precisely the required amount.

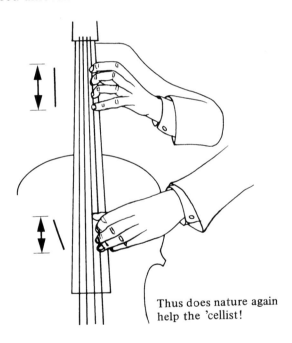

Thus does nature again
help the 'cellist!

But surely we must be free to choose any condition on any note from *senza vibrato* to a full-bodied oscillation, and, indeed, to run the gamut of vibrati on one and the same note if it is long enough! Without prejudice one way or the other, I think one should at least consider this latter possibility at the beginnings of the slow movements — the themes are mirror images of one another, amusingly — of the Boccherini B♭ and Haydn C major concertos. The long note followed by a group of shorter ones should 'burgeon', as it were, and flower into the succeeding notes. This follows an organic logic.

One can also imagine the reverse of this situation, where the long note might die away almost to extinction but at that point leading into dramatic spasms clearly articulated within a pianissimo.

In the case of the syllabic diminuendo (see vol. 1, p. 90) on a note of some length I believe that the vibrato should in general move from the wide–slow to the narrow–fast, thus maintaining a 'homeostasis', so to speak, of the intensity. If this be not done there is the danger that the diminuendo suggests a collapse. Of course, even the artistically intended collapse or shudder has its place.

I trust that this survey of the vibrato proves helpful. I reiterate that it is a personal business, and the reader must be encouraged to explore the regions I have *not* touched upon.

Vibrato is, in the last analysis, an Art, requiring, beyond sound craftsmanship, imagination, together with a sense of emotional logic and the development of a melody. The mechanical vibrato encountered in electric organs and vibraphones can have no place in 'cello technique, except where there is an intended irony.

# Positions I

I have come to look upon the traditional way of organizing the positions on the 'cello increasingly sourly; to think that it is unsound, both psychologically and cybernetically, and indeed that it is contrary to common sense.

A brief story may amuse you. I hope it does not.

I was asked to hear a *Wunderkind*. The boy played the Haydn C major concerto, which demands a mastery of every octave of the 'cello's tessitura. He seemed equally fluent in all parts of the instrument. I complimented him on having an enlightened teacher who had promoted this balanced development. 'On the contrary,' the boy said, 'I am forbidden to play in the thumb positions!' Then he added with a mischievous twinkle, 'but I do it anyway!'.

I believe that if a piano teacher were to say, 'Not higher than ♪ before the thirteenth birthday, not beyond ♪ before the eighteenth', he would not be the most sought-after person in the profession. Those of his pupils who remained loyal would be haunted by a phobia of the higher notes analogous to that of the higher positions (i.e. nearer the floor) on the 'cello suffered by gullible 'cellists. This fear is like an artificial neurosis induced by behaviouristic conditioning. By such means it is possible to induce a revulsion from peaches and cream!

I thought at first that this attitude was adopted by teachers wishing to keep their pupils for a lengthy period for commercial reasons. Even more unworthily, I thought that these teachers, having themselves been badly taught, had no wish for their phobias to be exposed, and thus restricted the pupil to areas where no such risk would be run. I then came to think that they were merely ignorant of cybernetics, and that into this vacuum there rushed moralistic ideas about doing one thing perfectly before moving on to another.

To play the 'cello in tune, let alone play it with subtlety and artistry, is to display a psycho-neuro-muscular expertise on the level of that of a brain surgeon or a diamond-splitter. This skill can most efficiently be acquired by the *progressive refinement of errors*. We must start by playing the WHOLE 'cello 'badly' – or, let us say, 'inexpertly'.

The 'upper' half of the 'cello has so much beauty; and here the fingering for all scales is the same, and, in any case, simple. A strong case could be made for starting people in the thumb positions and only when the hand is stretched and pliable enough, tackling the problems of the first position and its extensions! If nothing else, this would save elementary players from music of the 'Pixies at Dawn', 'Tulips at Twilight' variety!

Thus I propose four basic positions, rather like the camps established during a mountain climb, positions spread out along the whole tessitura of the 'cello and from which, after a period of familiarization, we may radiate.

I want to be conciliatory and so my first position is the same as the 'first' position we all know and love but, whereas the three others, the 'neck', 'viola' and 'violin' positions, are logically based, the first position has little but nostalgia to commend it. Do not forget that there is a position based upon *every note* on the 'cello! Furthermore, do not forget that there are vastly more notes on the 'cello than on the piano in the same compass.

In truth I dislike the use of the word 'position' in string-playing because of its suggestion, all too often palpably evident in the playing, of fixity. Anyway, there is a 'position' for every semitone, so the usual denotations are entirely arbitrary. The parallel use of the word 'position' on half the 'cello, to denote a static hand-placing, and the use of the same word to denote *all* the hand-placings for all the keys on the other half, is clearly absurd. One can logically speak of the thumb-positions, but of course these extend from one end of the 'cello to the other!

Naturally we must have a very clear idea of the interlocking 'grids' on the 'cello, and *at first* this is perhaps best established by holding down the whole hand position when playing, but, as described previously, this must eventually be abandoned in favour of the mentalizing of a 'cello-map, so to say.

Here are the four basic positions:

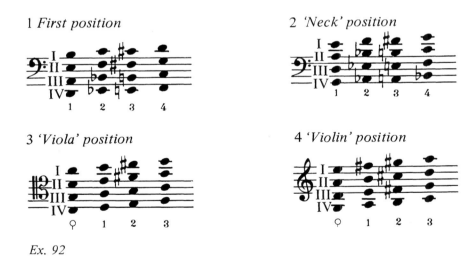

1 *First position*  2 *'Neck' position*

3 *'Viola' position*  4 *'Violin' position*

*Ex. 92*

We might describe this new way of organizing matters as the 'pythagorean' system. No. 3 is based on the half-string length. Nos. 2 and 4 are based on the one-third-string length. Nos. 1, 2, 3 and 4 are verifiable by testing with harmonics or open strings and are thus suitable for teaching to elementary players.

**Finding and testing the four basic positions**

1 *Testing the first position*

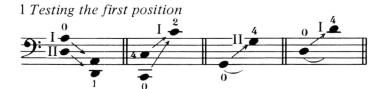

2 *Testing the 'neck' position*

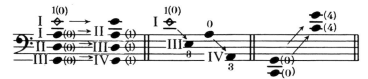

3 *Testing the 'viola' position*

4 *Testing the 'violin' position*

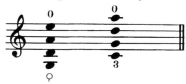

*Ex. 93*

One must place the thumb correctly. This placing assumes that the strings are true in fifths (i.e. that their cylindricality is intact and that therefore the mass per unit run is uniform). If one string only is involved the string should run 'through' the centre of the thumbnail. If two strings are involved the lower string runs through the thumbnail, the higher just to the right of the distal crease. This is to permit certain passages involving an alternation of fifths and tenths.

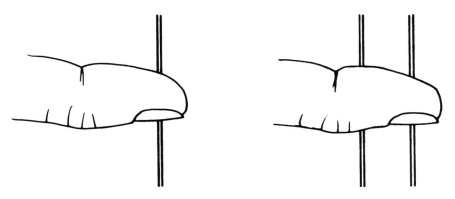

To reach other strings move the thumb across

Positions 1 and 2 are 'enveloped' by a minor third, 3 and 4 are enveloped by a fourth.

## Position-familiarization exercises

(without, and with, the bow)

*First position*

*Ex. 94*

I do not mark the bowings ⊓ or ∨. This is because one should alternately start the exercise ⊓ bow and ∨ bow. The principle of 'reduction of preferences' is of cardinal importance in all technical work.

*Ex. 95*

*Ex. 96*

'Neck' position

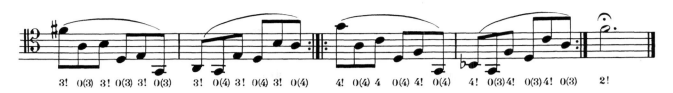

*Ex. 98*

*Ex. 99*

*Ex. 100*

To facilitate the familiarization of the 'viola' and the 'violin' positions, the third and fourth pythagorean positions, which differ from the two positions we have so far been exploiting in that they are both 'thumb' positions, I adopt procedures which may strike the blasé student as childish. Let that player laugh who has no residue of fear of the 'higher' positions. He has no need of me!

Now I have said that the 'viola' position, which we will consider as our *basic* thumb position, is itself based upon the half-string length, shown by Pythagoras to sound the octave above the fundamental. It is important that we can find this place beyond a peradventure. To this end I propose the following exercise which will, if nothing else, give rise to some merriment.

Ex. 101. Sound the open A and D strings with a down-bow, the left hand resting upon the left knee. Half-way through the bow-stroke place the thumb, in the manner shown on p. 60, on the half-string-length position, sounding the octaves above. On the up-bow again sound the open strings, this time placing the left hand on the top of the head! At the half-bow stroke again place the thumb at the half-string-length position. Then on the next down-bow stroke have the left hand on the side of the 'cello, and so forth. Repeat with the up-bow coinciding with the 'knee' position.

It is as well at first to employ the harmonics at the half-string-length position until this place is soundly established.

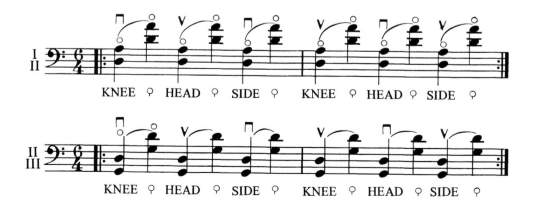

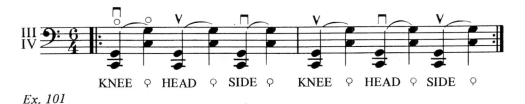

KNEE ♀ HEAD ♀ SIDE ♀ KNEE ♀ HEAD ♀ SIDE ♀

*Ex. 101*

At this point I want to introduce a fundamental concept, that of the 'grid' of the thumb positions. This grid is an imaginary cursor which, *keeping its relative values intact*, contracts and expands as it moves up and down the 'cello; and here we stumble again on one of those happy coincidences that bless the 'cello and its devotees. If we set the thumb across the datum, put the first finger a tone higher (on the lower of the two strings) the second a tone above that and the third, which dislikes separation from the second, a *semitone* above that, we have the first tetrachord of the major scale! Do the same on the upper string and you add the second tetrachord. What could be simpler or more natural? Further, this is the fingering for all the major keys in the thumb positions!

Thus the grid, in principle, looks like this:

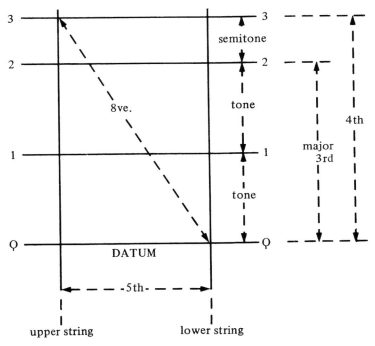

and, applied to the 'viola' position, like this.

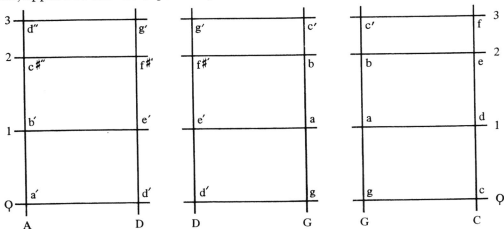

65

Starting at the right and moving to the left we can construct this curious, what I shall call 'pentatropic', scale, using the second tetrachord of the first octave as the first tetrachord of a new octave a fifth higher.

*Ex. 102*

As we approach the familiarization work for the two thumb-positions in our basic scheme I will remind you of the coincidence of the axiom of G.K. Chesterton with the insights of cybernetics and suggest that slowish trills of ever-increasing error-refinement may bring us the most rapidly to that haven where we would be. The reason for slowish trills is that fast ones land us in the complications about aural illusions. Thus the fast trill on a tone interval *sounds* flatter than it is, and sounds increasingly flat as the speed of trilling is increased. (See p. 158 below.)

As before, deny the fingers, at this stage, the advantage of hand movements. This is perhaps especially relevant to the use of the third finger. Make the fingers themselves do some work, keeping them somewhat rounded.

It is easy to derive material for exercises on the middle two strings (the centre grid) — merely substitute:

*Ex. 103*

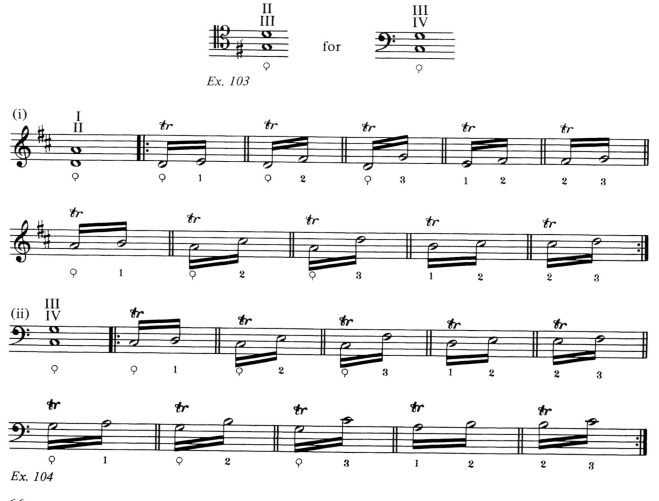

*Ex. 104*

*Ex. 105*

Sometimes accent the first and fourth ♪'s ( $\frac{6}{16}$ ), sometimes the first and fifth ( $\frac{3}{8}$ ).

*Ex. 106*

*Ex. 107*

*This Old Man*

*This Old Man*

*Ex. 108*

*Brahms, Lullaby*

*Brahms, Lullaby*

*Ex. 109*

*Pẽr Spelmann* (Norwegian Folk-tune)

*Pẽr Spelmann*

*Ex. 110*

*Die zwey alten Geyger*

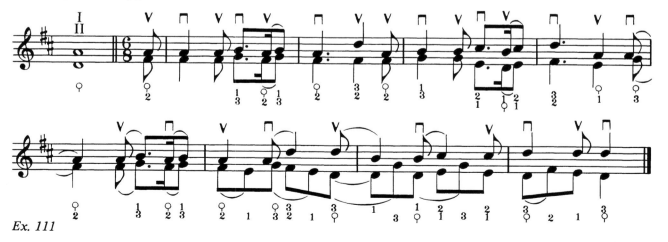

*Ex. 111*

70

The familiarization-work in the fourth pythagorean position, the 'violin' position is analogous to that in the third. As always, check your posture and body-use. No wild contortions are required to lay one's hand naturally into this position. Keep the shoulders low, move the arms from their sockets under the clavicle.

One point may be worrisome to players with large fingers. The distance between the finger-pads when the fingers are held closely together may still be greater than a semitone. The solution is to let one finger fall on to the spot it should occupy, whilst the other moves smartly out of the way. When one begins to cultivate a taste for the small semitone (see p. 153, below) this technique acquires even greater importance.

Naturally this makes a clear trill of the semitone in this position unlikely for the fat-fingered. Fortunately there is a solution to this problem which I will divulge at the appropriate time. If I did so now, it would render turgid that which should be becoming ever clearer.

The next exercise establishes the datum of the 'violin' position (at one-third-string-length). As before, use harmonics at first.

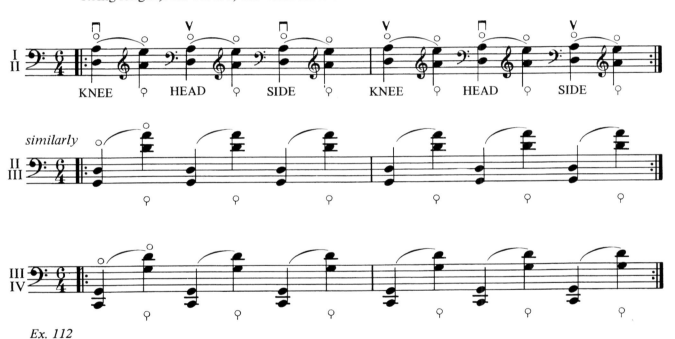

*Ex. 112*

The following may also be found valuable:

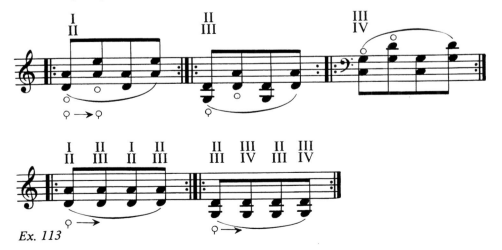

*Ex. 113*

Check again the generalized thumb-positions grid (p. 65 above), noting the fingerings and the interval relationships. Applying this to the 'violin' position we derive:

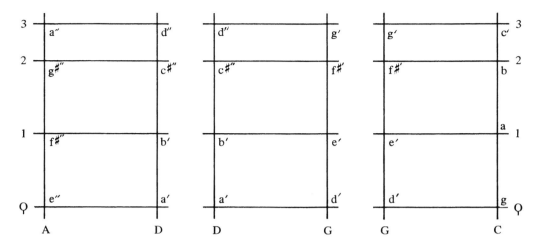

Our pentatropic scale will now be:

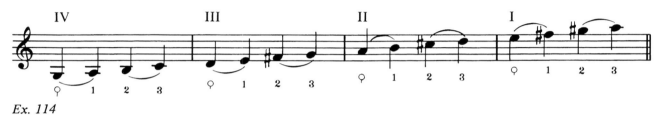

*Ex. 114*

Now in the interest of economy I propose a novel scheme. We are going to adapt the material deployed for the familiarization of the 'viola' position to similar use for the 'violin' position. For exercises on the upper two strings we merely take the second half of Exx. 104, 105 etc. and substitute:

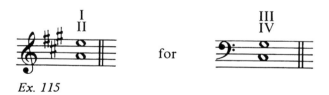

*Ex. 115*

For the middle two strings we take the first half of Exx. 104 and 105, and substitute:

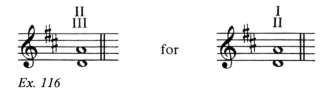

*Ex. 116*

and for the lower two strings we take the second half and substitute:

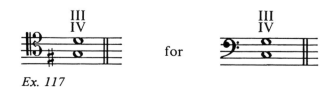

*Ex. 117*

72

In the initial study, omit the semitone trills unless your fingers are thin.

The fact that this clef and key-signature substitution is possible underlines the logical simplicity of this 'new' pythagorean system.

As I intend *Die zwey alten Geyger* to be played on the upper two strings, I must here provide the relevant transposition so that these old gentlemen may aspire to higher things!

*Die zwey alten Geyger* ('violin' position)

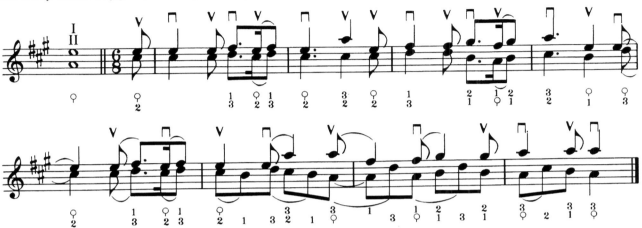

*Ex. 118*

Now the familiarization work we have been doing in the 'viola' and 'violin' positions has so far lacked the lateral linking feature I have provided on the 'first' and 'neck' positions, and I think an analogous set of exercises might be of service.

**Lateral linking in the 'viola' position**
(first revise the relevant pentatropic scale, p. 66, above)

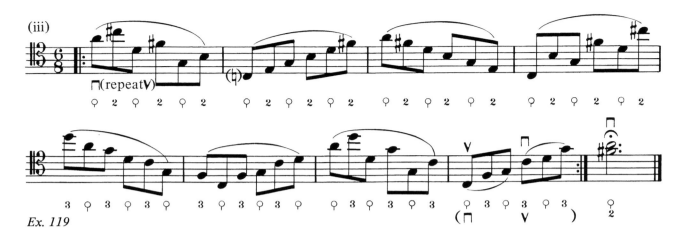

Ex. 119

## Lateral linking in the 'violin' position

(first revise the relevant pentatropic scale, p. 72 above)

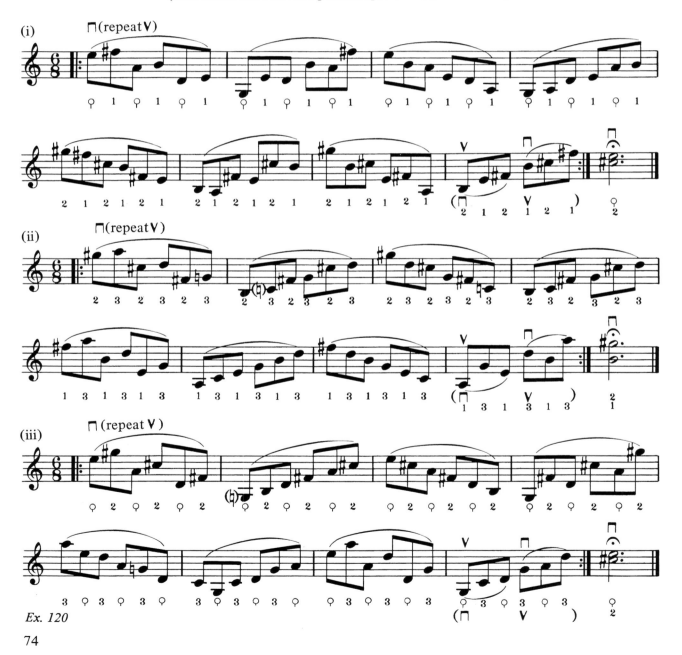

Ex. 120

Now I have spoken of, and described, the four basic positions, from which we will get our bearings for all the others. They are certainly within the competence of most 'cellists, even those of tender years or modest ambition.

As an appendix to these four I want to add a fifth position for those with a little more ambition. This is no more than that position based upon the quarter-string-length, producing the double octave.

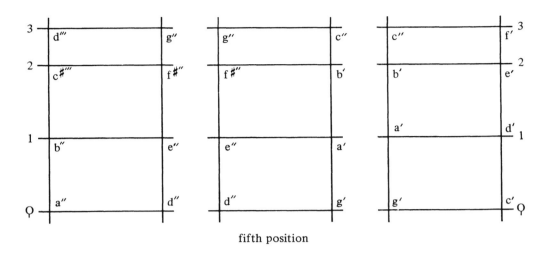

fifth position

The pentatropic scale will be:

*Ex. 121*

In order to familiarize oneself with this position, play the material of the viola position an octave higher. Again work the knee, head, side exercise and linking exercises analogous to those between positions three and four. Link with both these positions.

Having now set up a reliable 'navigational' system we will for the moment turn our attention to a related topic, but with the intention of returning later.

# Shifting I

As we have at the most five digits with which to make the notes on the 'cello, we have to move the hand around, and we call it 'shifting'. Now we can differentiate between two species of shift: (i) the functional, and (ii) the expressive.

In the past, there were players who did not make this distinction. They would use every shift as an opportunity for an 'expressive' slide careless of any artistic logic. The effect through modern ears of this manner of playing is usually emetic.

My feeling is that, as with the Bowing Regime (vol. 1, p. 33), the policy should be to acquire a reliable technique that is artistically neutral, and then move on to the exploration of the artistic possibilities. Calculation is anathema to the 'amateur' who cares so little for the nature of his beloved that he is content to be ignorant of her nature. In an *artist*, whether amateur or professional, calculation joins hands with sincerity and intuition.

Thus from the functional standpoint we must be able to shift cleanly, as cleanly as does a pianist, and from the expressive standpoint we must study, *and bring to the point of replicability,* the panoply of portamenti which is one of the glories of the violoncello.

Surely, the *whole point* of dispensing with keys and frets *is* the portamento. Otherwise all we have is an inadequate instrument whose only advantages over the piano are the ability to make a crescendo on one note, and to control the rate of diminuendo.

Now, I think the best way to work our way into a good technique of functional shifting is by means of finger-substitutions on the same note.

Take any note high enough to be managed by the fourth finger, write it out many times and then 'finger' it arbitrarily, thus:

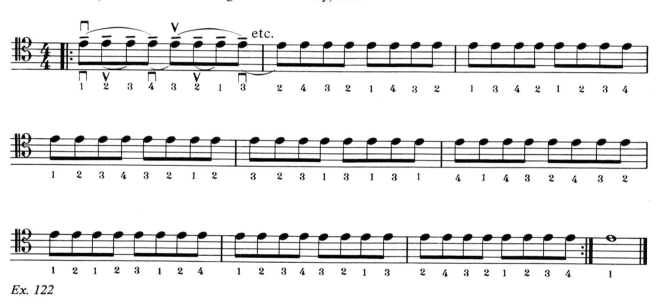

Ex. 122

Take a different note on a different string at each practice session. Give a good percussion on each note: real finger-substitution, not 'smearing'.

The next step might well be:

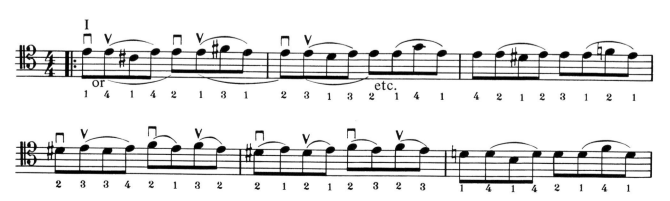

*Ex. 123*

Repeat, reversing the bowing.* Repeat on the D string, substituting the bass clef for the tenor, B♮s for B♯s, and B♭s for B♮s.

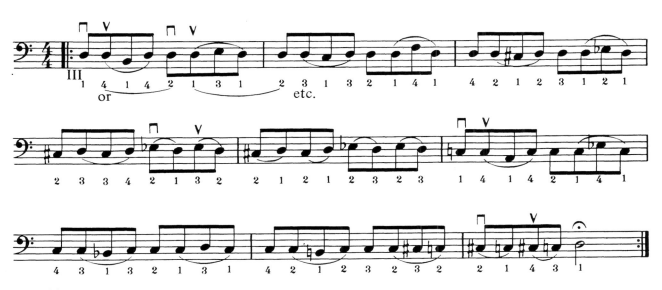

*Ex. 124*

A cardinal point is that one must often make hand movements at a speed *unrelated* to the pulse of the music. However slowly you practise the foregoing the shifts should be executed rapidly. See also discussion of downward shifting (p. 107 below).

*Ex. 125*

* On the principle of 'Reduction of Preferences' – a prime aim – *always* do this wherever possible.

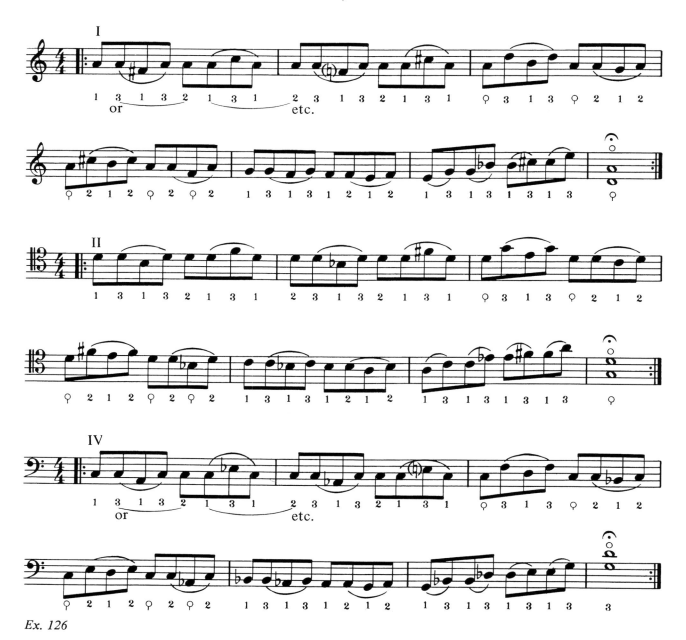

*Ex. 126*

The case occurs frequently in scales when we must perforce play adjacent notes with a fingering that is *opposite* to the 'rational' one. Practising of this manoeuvre is both essential and customarily neglected. I will defer a close description of the downward shifting mechanism until a little later (p. 107).

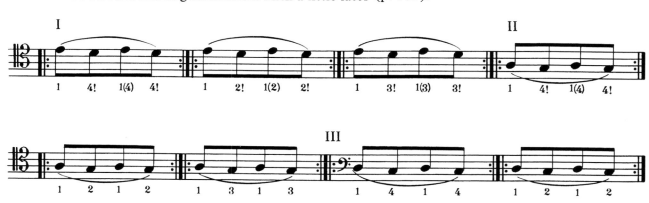

*Ex. 127*

Practise the above with the single bars repeated, and also taking two and three bars together in one bow.

Compound it also with:

*Continuing:*

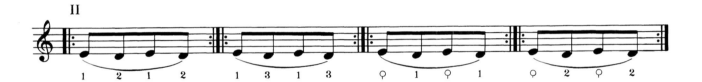

*Ex. 128*

Practise the bars separately, as before, but also together; two, three and four. Also compound this with:

*Ex. 129*

*Ex. 130*

# Positions II

Now I think at this point that you could justly accuse me of slipping in something on the sly! I have, in the guise of studying functional shifts, moved your hand into positions other than the four basic, or parent, positions.

For those who like strong reference-points we will go back to these parent positions and derive two offspring for each of them. Of course we can play the material already deployed for each position several semitones either side, and I hope that your initiative is strong enough to have suggested to you this course, but I will here indulge myself to the extent of providing fresh material.

### Offspring of the first position

(i) *One semitone pegwards* – the so-called 'half'-position

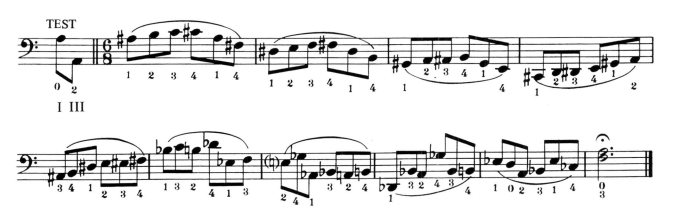

*Ex. 131*

You will notice that I do not always include the notation denoting percussion and plucking for the left hand. I economize in this way on the assumption that by now your kinetic touch is fully operational.

(ii) *One semitone bridgewards*

*Ex. 132*

You will notice that I veer half-way through each exercise from the 'sharp-side' to the 'flat-side'. When you have tasted the delights of Creative Intonation (p. 152 below), this will mean something significant to you, but, for the moment, just play equitemperamentally! After all, you have also to be able to do this on those occasions when you must mix with the lower orders – the pianists – for the sake of playing sonatas and such!

*The Left Hand*

## Offspring of the 'neck' position (p. 59 above)

(i) *One semitone pegwards*

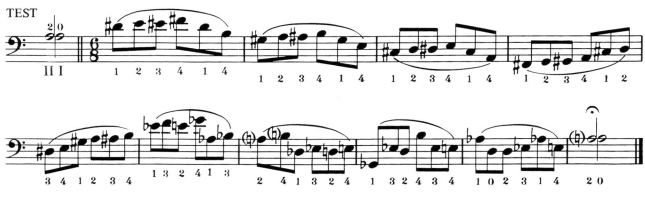

Ex. 133

Now revise the 'neck' position. Then:

(ii) *One semitone bridgewards*

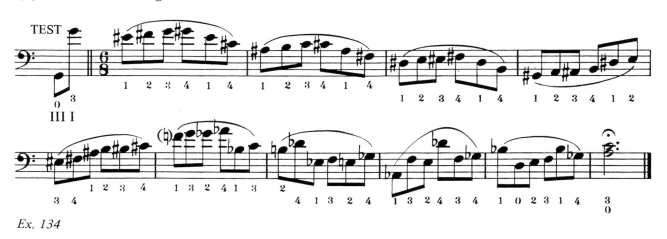

Ex. 134

## Offspring of the 'viola' position (p. 59 above)

(i) *One semitone pegwards*

Ex. 135

82

Now revise the 'viola' position. Then:

(ii) *One semitone bridgewards*

*Ex. 136*

## Offspring of the 'violin' position (p. 59 above)

(i) *One semitone pegwards*

*Ex. 137*

Now revise the 'violin' position. Then:

(ii) *One semitone bridgewards*

*Ex. 138*

You will notice that there remain a few positions, based (on the A string) on:

*Ex. 137*

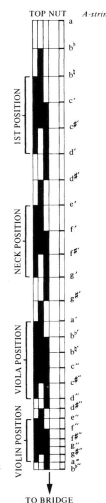

We will call these the 'cousin' positions. Exercises on these follow, but, as will be seen in the accompanying diagram, based for the sake of clarity on the A string, we have already covered every note from ♮ to ♮ and introduced a logical scheme for navigation within this range. We see that as the gaps between the 'parent' positions are two semitones wide in every case, these are neatly bridged by the bridgeward offspring of the lower position linking with the pegward offspring of the higher.

I am convinced that there are enormous advantages to be derived from the adoption of this system as a *basis* of our knowledge of the 'topography' of the 'cello. Naturally we will, as we gain experience, employ exotic genera of fingerings not to be classified. We will delight in these with greater *élan* if we have a firm basis from which to depart.

For the sake of simplicity equal temperament notation is here employed, but see page 152, 'Creative Intonation'.

## Exercises for the cousin positions

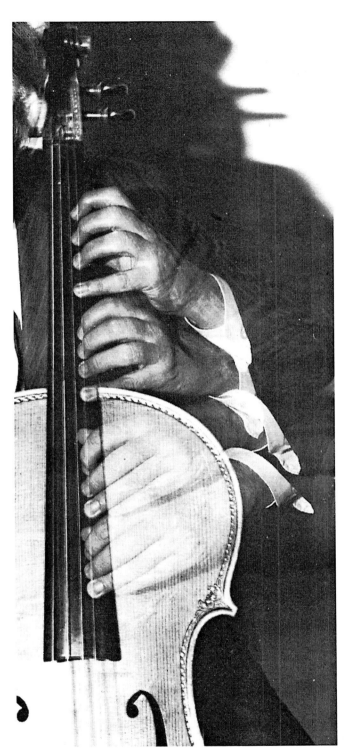

The left hand shown in the four basic positions

*Ex. 138*

# Shifting II

I am interlarding material about shifting and that about positions because these two factors are so closely interrelated in actual practice. I suppose one could say that shifting relates to the longitudinal aspect and positions to the lateral.

I feel it would now be a good idea to make a longitudinal link between the positions already described, and to this end I introduce the idea of the 'ergonomic scale'; that is to say, a scale tailored to hand and arm convenience rather than to musical contingencies. We will move into more musical scales by and by. Practise taking two notes to the bow, and also three. Occasionally, with the motive of gaining ever greater control, why not experiment with a mixture of twos and threes, thus grouping the notes into $\frac{5}{8}$ bars?

## Longitudinal ergonomic scale no. 1

( ♀0 means 'start the note with the thumb "full-stopping" the string, releasing onto the harmonic mode just before shifting'. Upon ascending one may, if desired, take the ♀ on the harmonic at first.)

Ex. 139

Ex. 140

# The Left Hand

## Exercises in Longitudinal ergonomic scale no. 1

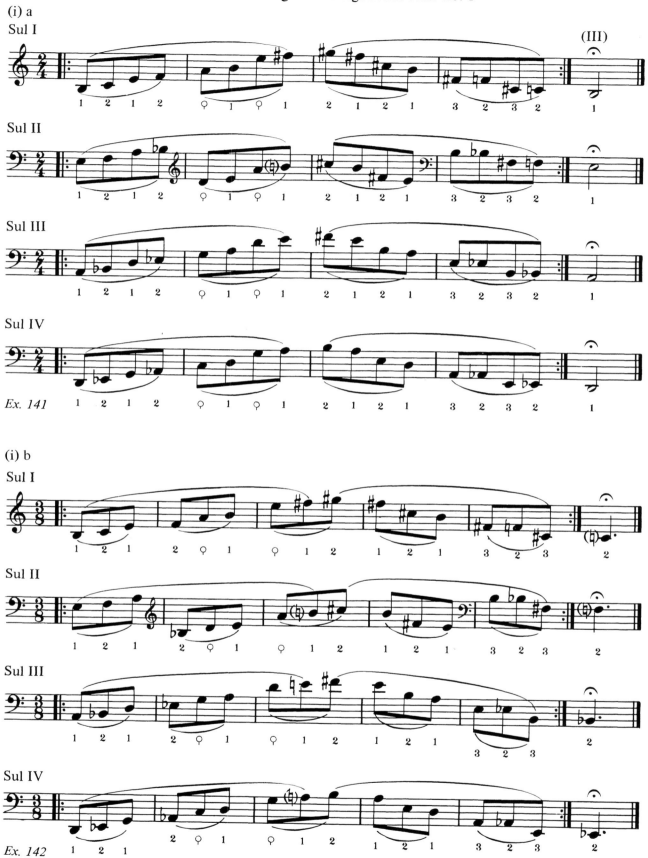

(i) a
Sul I
Sul II
Sul III
Sul IV

*Ex. 141*

(i) b
Sul I
Sul II
Sul III
Sul IV

*Ex. 142*

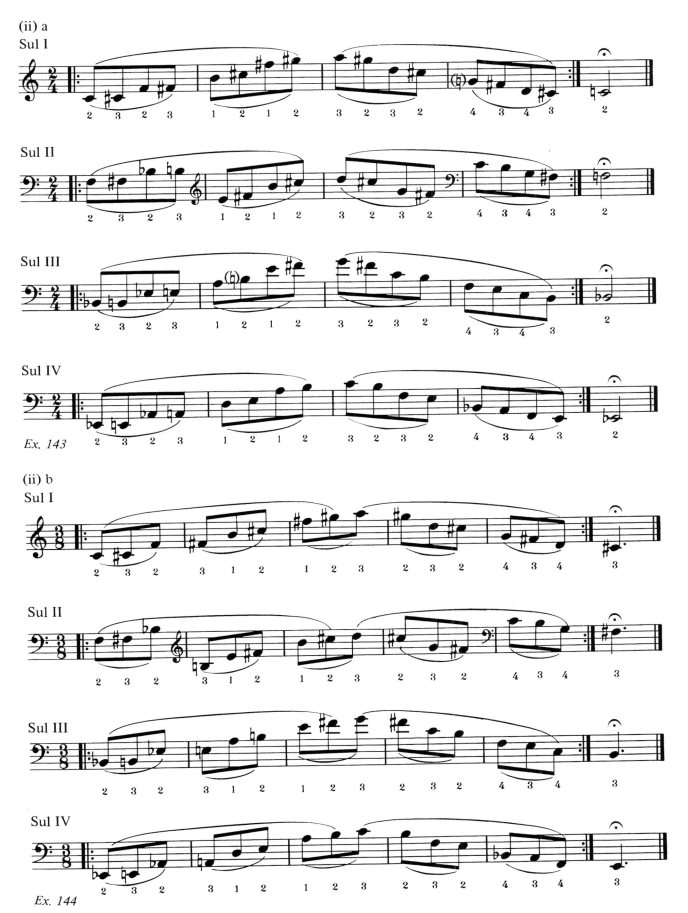

Ex. 143

Ex. 144

# Positions III

We will now take a look at extended positions in the first and 'neck' positions, and their relatives! As usually understood, the extended position is based on the ability of the first and second fingers to tolerate a greater separation than can the others. In the positions near the top-nut only the stretch 1 to 2 is really capable of providing the interval of the tone between adjacent fingers. This does not mean that I do not welcome the inspired ideas of Joachim Stutschewsky, but the student should be cautioned to proceed with his stretches between fingers 3 and 4, and more particularly, between fingers 2 and 3, with circumspection and by slow stages.

Only those players with exceptionally large, supple and trained hands should attempt to play the interval of a tone in the lower positions with the second and third fingers. Please heed this warning.

So, the first position extended is thus:

*Ex. 145*

and the extension of the 'neck' position:

*Ex. 146*

Let us accustom ourselves to the 1 to 2 stretch of a tone in both these extensions of the parent positions.

1(a)

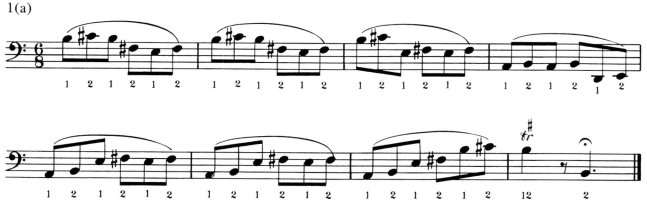

90

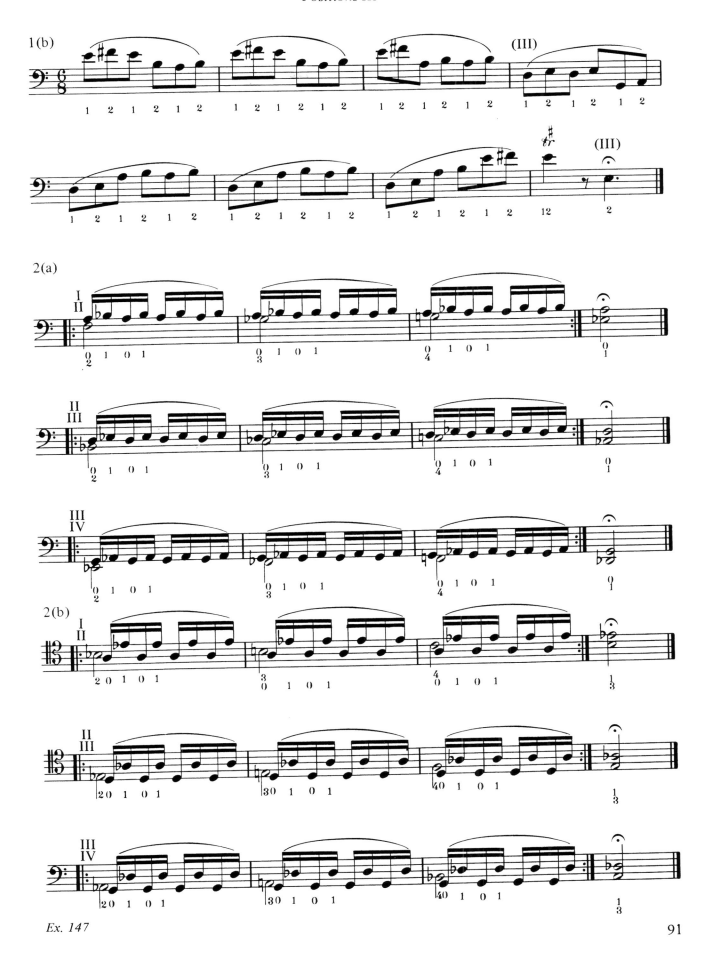

Ex. 147

And so to exercises in the extensions of the first and 'neck' positions.

It is very important to drive from one's mind any idea that the word 'extension' implies anything abnormal. It is merely a word customarily used to denote a certain 'lay' of the hand.

If you experience difficulty in articulating the music in these exercises, you should perhaps do further training, using the 'bridging' exercises (p. 15 above).

Ex. 148

And now we exercise in the 'offspring' positions of the extended first position and the extended 'neck' position.

## Offspring of First-(ext) position

(i) *One semitone pegwards*

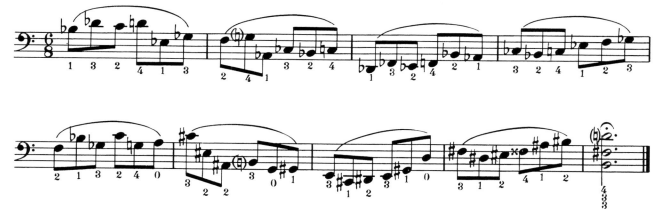

(ii) *One semitone bridgewards*

**Offspring of the Neck-(ext) position**

(i) *One semitone pegwards*

(ii) *One semitone bridgewards*

*Ex. 149*

We will exercise in the two 'cousin' positions (extended) found between the first
and the 'neck' positions and their offspring.

*Ex. 150*

# Zig-Zags

Before we proceed further let's have a 'fun interlude'. Let's crash through all the positions in oblique motion across the strings, using finger-substitutions. Perhaps I can introduce here the idea of the 'equivalent semitone', which is simply an interval played on two strings which if the fingers had taken up the same position on *one* string would sound as a semitone. Thus the 'equivalent semitone' is either a minor sixth or an augmented fourth – the dreaded 'tritone'. I do not trot out this idea to complicate matters, but merely because many people find it helpful.

*Zig-zagging by 'equivalent semitones'*

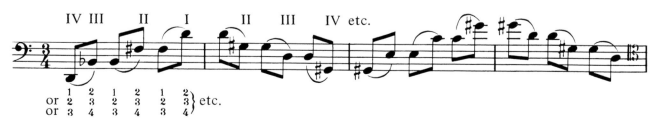

IV III

AND BACK!

AND BACK!

*Zig-zagging by 'equivalent tones'*

or $\frac{1}{2}$ $\frac{3}{4}$ $\frac{1}{2}$ $\frac{3}{4}$ $\frac{1}{2}$ $\frac{3}{4}\}$ etc.            $\frac{1}{2}$ $\frac{2}{3}$ $\frac{1}{2}$ $\frac{2}{3}$ $\frac{1}{2}$ $\frac{2}{3}$   $\frac{0}{0}$ (III)
                                                                                                         (IV)

**AND BACK!**

or $\frac{2}{3}$ $\frac{1}{2}$ $\frac{2}{3}$ $\frac{1}{2}$ $\frac{2}{3}$ $\frac{1}{2}\}$ $\{\frac{3}{4}$ $\frac{1}{2}$ $\frac{3}{4}$ $\frac{1}{2}$   $\frac{3}{4}$ $\frac{1}{2}\}$ etc.

**AND BACK!**

*Ex. 151*

# Shifting III

We can now derive a second species of longitudinal ergonomic scale.

Sul I

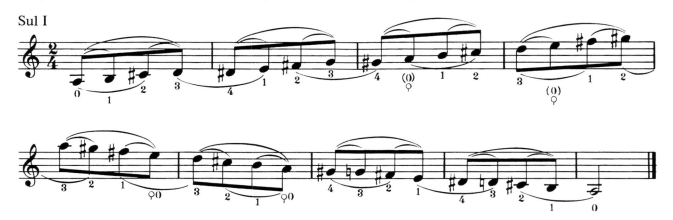

*Ex. 152*

Thus, we coyly approach the major scale by merely excising two notes:

Sul II

Sul III

Sul IV

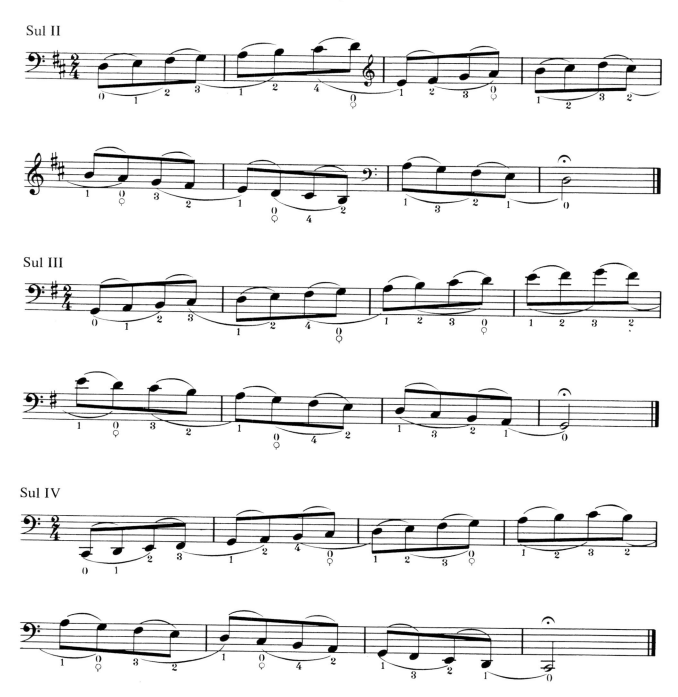

*Ex. 153*

Now I must make it clear that I am not proposing this fingering as a substitute for more familiar ones. I propose it as a useful exercise in linking the four basic positions and in familiarizing oneself in a certain 'set' of the hand.

This might be the moment to deploy an amusing conceit: a universal fingering for scales on one string. Again this must not be taken as a challenger to the more usual fingerings. Do not employ it in the harmonic minor scale. The formula is thus: $x$ 12 12 123  12 12 123; where $x$ is either 0, 1, 2, 3, 4, or ♀.

For example:

Sul II

and return.

*Ex. 154*

As always in the thumb positions, the thumb should rest upon the string, and preferably on the position of a note consciously known, often a fourth lower in pitch than the note played by the third finger (keeping the grid pattern).

In parentheses I would like to say that although it is unorthodox I sometimes put my thumb *underneath* the fingerboard in the higher positions on lower strings in a slow tempo. I am thinking especially of the slow movement of Shostakovich's Sonata in D minor, Opus 40. Towards the end of Max Bruch's *Kol Nidrei* the same idea is helpful.

Now the fingering which appears in Longitudinal Ergonomic scale no. 2 is of fundamental importance.

*Ex. 155*

It is the basis of the 'modern' fingering where the tone surmounted by the semi-tone is involved. I say 'modern', but it has been in use for over a century and there is some evidence of it in the eighteenth century! But in the backwoods its use is still the occasion of raised eyebrows.

If one traces the linkage of the upper arm and the forearm-hand complex (we have, I trust, agreed that for the basic singing vibrato the forearm and hand must substantially work as one unit), we find that:

*Ex. 156*

falls naturally under the hand, and increasingly so as the left hand approaches the bridge, whereas the conformation 1 3 4 becomes increasingly less favourable. Indeed the 'higher' one goes with the irrational fingering the more does the body-use become rigid. An artificial 'kink' must be introduced at the wrist which has a most unfortunate effect upon the vibrato and puts a strain upon the neck.

What could be more cheironomically sound than the taking of the semitone precisely with those two fingers that prefer not to be separated! Then the addi-tion of another semitone, played by the fourth finger, gives the major third between 1 and 4, embracing the two tones 1, 2 and 2, 4. This last, of course, applies more usually to the 'lower' positions. In the thumb positions we would base our fingering upon the ♀123 conformation, but, again, it is often necessary to use the fourth finger. This use of the fourth finger in the thumb positions arises mainly in the case of the music of contemporary composers, most of whom appear

99

to consider it beneath their dignity to acquaint themselves with the nature of the instruments they write for. If they are anything they are pianists, and tend to write for a five-note hand-grouping rather than a four-note one.

Another advantage of the 'lay' of the hand we have been examining is that one is thus ready to go up into the 'higher' positions with conviction and force if need be. The backwoods fingering prevents this and one is obliged to *drag* the hand upwards. Not much music is improved by this sluggardly proceeding.

Of course one must be careful in invoking the word 'natural' in all this. All fine playing involves training and continued exercise to maintain strength and suppleness. Also, suitable fingering is always a matter of context.

There is no fingering logic that covers all scales, except perhaps in the thumb positions, but how often in a practical context does one play a complete scale of several octaves? A few examples come to mind, but in each of these an 'unusual' fingering must be deployed if the artistic problems are to be resolved imaginatively.

In Beethoven's A major sonata Opus 69, in the first movement, it would be unwise to employ the 'usual' fingering for the E major scale because, owing to the lazy hankering after the 'lower' positions, there would be large leaps and stretches giving rise to a certain disjointedness. By going 'higher' before crossing strings these gaps can be reduced and the natural flow of the phrase be promoted. I always think of this scale as the stem of a tulip, the sap rising and nourishing the song of the flower. With a bad fingering the stem becomes a dry twisted stick which would not even support a plastic flower!

Thus let us take these fingerings and bowings:

**Allegro, ma non tanto**

*Ex. 157*

Take care to approach with the bow the new string towards the end of the last note on the old one, again with the motive of avoiding bumps and unwanted accents. At the end of the fifth note, B, played on the C string with the fourth finger, point the first finger back towards the pegbox, thus reducing the leap and providing the basis for a fluid cheironomic *enchaînement*. To the same end, place the thumb back to a position where it can act as a pivot between 1 and 4.

It is important to make an 'anti-accent' on the open A string. If one really applies oneself to the acquiring of intimate note-control on the same point-of-contact, as advocated in this book, there should be no problem. Notice where the bowing is 'asymmetrical' in order to conceal the downbeat and where symmetrical to give a slight feeling of poised weight on the downbeat.

In Elgar's Concerto in E minor Opus 85, in the first movement, the soloist executes an E minor ascending scale of extraordinary *élan* and increasing tension, bringing in the first orchestral tutti on the topmost note. If the upper octave of this scale be fingered 12 12 123, as would probably be considered orthodox, the downbeats would coincide with the shifts rather than with percussed notes, thus weakening the rhythm and decisiveness at a crucial moment. Thus we must take the fingering:

*Ex. 158*

There is an additional advantage in taking two 3s at the top of the scale. Conductors vary in their ability to bring in an orchestra, tutti, after a predominantly solo passage. It is essential for the soloist to be especially aware at this moment and place his note squarely with the orchestra's chord. Make sure that the Gs in the scale are not too sharp to express the soul of E minor, the key of the scale and of the concerto.

Similar to this but faster is a scale that occurs in Dvořák's Concerto in B minor Opus 104, in the last movement. The two 3s appear again in an analogous position and for the same reason. The rest of the fingering derives from a wish to reduce the number of shifts to a minimum.

*Ex. 159*

# Delay – an interlude

I would like to interpose here a brief note upon the value of delay. This might more suitably be found in a discussion of artistic, as distinct from technical, matters, but many a purely technical problem will yield to the procedure I will now outline.

The difficulty is that one must presuppose a wakefulness that, I am persuaded, is a very rare commodity. Much 'cello-playing has as its impulse the wish to defend oneself against the acerbities of raw experience, to wrap oneself in a cocoon of pleasant sound, or to flee into frenzied activity. In this case this commodity of wakefulness is bound to be absent.

However, let us optimistically assume that there is indeed a captain on the bridge. One must be able to say at any moment: 'Stop! . . . not now . . . NOW!', the time between the 'not now' and the 'NOW' being infinitesimal but vital. I am sure there is no coincidence in the fact that Casals was fascinated by the teachings of Bergson. In this infinitesimal moment the initiative has been grasped and thus what is subsequently done is done consciously, with decision and impact.

Quite often a technical failure is due to the 'carrying forward' of building-up physical tensions, probably based upon a false muscular analogy with increasing musical tension, together with an associated mental vagueness – a lack of ego.

The conscious direction of all that is going on would ideally be present continually, but some of its accruing benefits can be stolen, so to say, by splitting up any passage that is being practised into its components. Then, during re-assembly, the temporal disjointedness can be progressively reduced to zero whilst retaining the clarity of the continuum of associated and essential mental events.

But the vital thing is that, at nodal moments, what is done should be done *consciously* and at a *chosen* instant. This instant can often profitably be fractionally later than a sleepwalker would play it, and yet the delay can be imperceptible to an audience except in the appreciation that they are in the hands of a master.

Theodor Reik has pointed out that in German the word 'Takt' means both a sense of correctness and a musical bar or measure. Thus we get an added dimension to our concept of tact. Tact implies not only the saying or doing of the right thing, but also that it be said or done at the right time, this in turn depending upon that condition of wakefulness that we have posited as a *sine qua non*.

Let us return to our consideration of scales *in vitro*. After a little training the following will be found comfortable:

*Ex. 160*

Practise the descent also.

In such a case as:

*Ex. 161*

it is clearly bad practice to employ the backwoods fingering 41414141; see what happens after eight bars! Use rather 41314131 which leaves the basic hand position undisturbed. Apart from training, it is by paying attention to cheironomic logic that one can improve dramatically the technical standard of one's playing.

We must plan intelligently. From the foregoing principles we might play:

*Ex. 162*

but clearly, in the context:

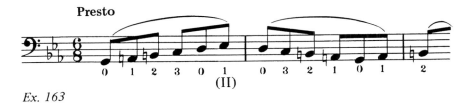

*Ex. 163*

there is a gross misfingering, and we should better have used 013401043101, making an extension between 4 and 1. Of course it is evident that this example can be fingered in other ways: (i) sul III, (ii) sul IV, or (iii) lying across IV and III.

But certainly we should accustom ourselves to this creative conformation of the left hand. To promote this, let us therefore construct a third ergonomic scale.

(i) shift-interval of a semitone

Sul I

*Ex. 164*

Practise in the bowings indicated, but also in six- and nine-note groupings, so that shifts and bow-changes do not always coincide. Practise also in four and eight, and five and ten-note groupings. Thus:

Sul I

etc.

Sul I

etc.

*Ex. 165*

(ii) shift-interval of a tone

Sul I

Sul II

Sul III

**Sul IV**

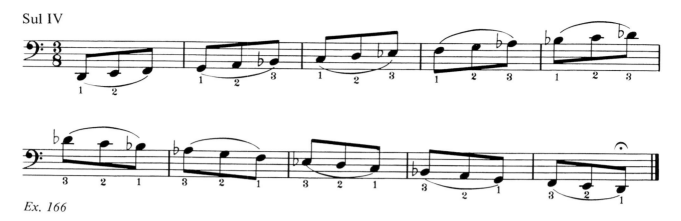

*Ex. 166*

As before, practise in the bowings indicated and also in six- and nine-note groupings and also in four- and eight-note groupings and five- and ten-note groupings.

When one has this kind of 'pile' of positions it is often a good idea to practise the movement of the first finger separately:

*Movement of the first finger in Ex. 164*
(A pile of major thirds)  Practise similarly on the other strings

**Sul I**

*Ex. 167*

*Movement of the first finger in Ex. 166*
(A pile of fourths)  Practise similarly on the other strings

**Sul I**

*Ex. 168\**

I think it would be found to be of great benefit to rework the two forms of this longitudinal ergonomic scale substituting ♀ 12 for 123. Practise also the two 'piles' substituting ♀ for 1. One must not forget that the ♀ positions extend from one end of the 'cello to the other. I only use the word 'position' in this context because it is the custom. In reality it is a misnomer.

I have previously (p. 75) made a distinction between functional and expressive shifting. Now in the case of the upward shift the functional shift is usually executed by a very rapid movement along the string of the hand and finger, the speed of this movement being unrelated to the tempo of the music. I am at present speaking of consecutive shifting. The following would require a different approach:

* *Patinages* (Cambridge University Press, 1982) will be found relevant to the above two exercises.

106

*Ex. 169*

The metamorphosis of a functional upward shift to an expressive one is largely a matter of degree. The ingredients to be balanced are the speed of shift, vibrato, crescendo or diminuendo and so forth (see p. 113).

But with the downward shift the distinction is more clear-cut. It is my opinion that very few players should attempt the expressive downward shift. The results of a miscalculation here are far more disastrous than those arising from a mis-judged upward portamento. But, *per contra*, it must be said that the refined down-ward expressive portamenti of such masters as Heifetz or Menuhin, not to mention Yvonne Printemps, are perhaps the most subtle and emotional of the weapons in their artistic armouries.

However this may be, all of us, perforce, must deploy a reliable technique of downward shifting. Let us first examine two ways, commonly encountered, of going about it in the wrong way.

The first wrong way has at least the excuse that it can be used to help beginners find their way around! But crutches must be thrown away as soon as possible, that is to say as soon as the mentalized 'cello-map has become adequately clear.

*Wrong way no. 1*

*Ex. 170*

is manifestly a crude way of playing:

*Ex. 171*

Another wrong way one frequently encounters is reminiscent of a landing aero-plane, the finger sliding downward from above in a dreadful smearing glissando.

*Wrong way no. 2*

*Ex. 172*

Of course one should practise these examples in order to extend one's command of the medium. It is always a good idea to practise inadequate solutions, even mistakes, in order to exorcize gremlins. It may be that by practising this last fault you may arrive at a degree of control that will open the way to a delicate and sensuous downward portamento, either on the one finger or proceeding from one finger to another. But always remember that, artistically speaking, you are playing with fire!

How then should we make the downward shift? The first thing is to sort out our psychophysical notions. The pitch-movement may be downward, but the action is upward! We must make an effort against gravity, and thus are deprived of an advantage we enjoy when making an 'upward' (floorwards) shift. The body-use is crucial, but I have nothing new to say on this. The body must be disposed as has been described (vol. 1, p. 83). The body weight must be supported by the chair and not the 'cello. The arm and hand weight must then be available for total or partial use. The left humero-scapula joint must be free.

Now practise the following, giving a very strong percussion on the second E♭ :

*Ex. 173*

All we have to do if we want these notes

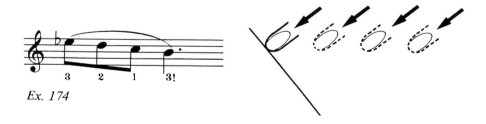

*Ex. 174*

is, *from the fingers' point of view*, to execute the same movements as before but to 'outwit' the third finger by smartly moving the hand back so that it hits B instead of E♭. It is all very simple but takes a little practise. Remember the principle that we must sometimes make gestures at a speed unrelated to the tempo of the music. This is a case in point.

At the start of the fall of the third finger, the finger is aimed at E♭ but at the completion of the hand movement it finds itself on B. The motion is unlike that of the aeroplane mentioned above, it is more like that of a helicopter! Check your body-use and make sure you permit free breathing at the crucial moment.

We will now apply the foregoing principle in some exercises:

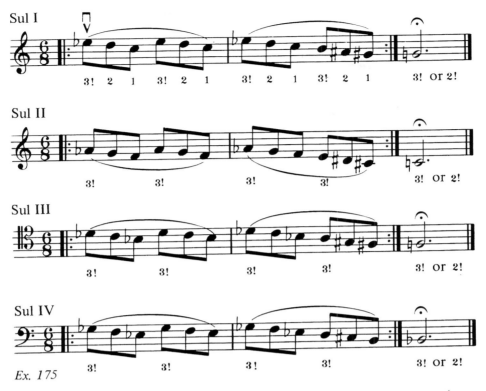

Ex. 175

It would be profitable to repeat the exercise with the fingering pattern: 2! 1 ♀ .

It is always useful to practise the nodal point of difficulty and then integrate the improved functioning into the whole. Remember Frank Merrick's dictum 'Plan, play, judge'. Don't censor the left-hand bowing mistakes with a bowing trick!

Practise, slowly at first: (♪ = 100)

then:

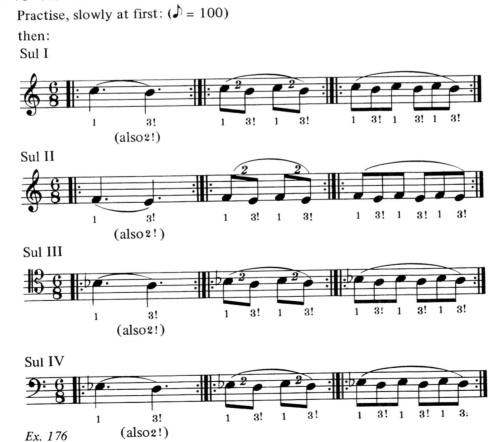

Ex. 176    (also 2!)

Especial care should be taken to ensure that the functional downward shift to the fourth finger is clean. Check that the finger is acting correctly, the distal phalanx always pointing at the note, joints flexing and the hand uninvolved (see p. 4).

Practise, slowly at first:

then,

I have been kind in making the shift interval a semitone, but clearly we must also work with larger intevals. Work also all the examples on different notes.

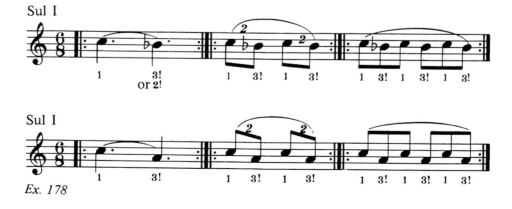

*Ex. 178*

and similarly on the other strings.

*Ex. 179*

and similarly on the other strings.

I would like to remind you of the important point that one must frequently make movements of the hand that are not related to the pulse of the music. Thus, here, when practising the exercises at different tempi from slow to fast, see to it that the shifting is always rapid. To promote this end, see to it that the psychosomatic preconditions are present. If, as you should, you occasionally practise the exercises *pp*, make sure that there is nothing 'soft' about the left-hand mechanics. There is some truth in the old dictum — 'the left hand must always play *forte*!' I certainly feel that clarity becomes especially important in quiet music.

Here is another exercise to highlight the problem we are dealing with. Keep the thumb in the neck of the 'cello until this is no longer possible:

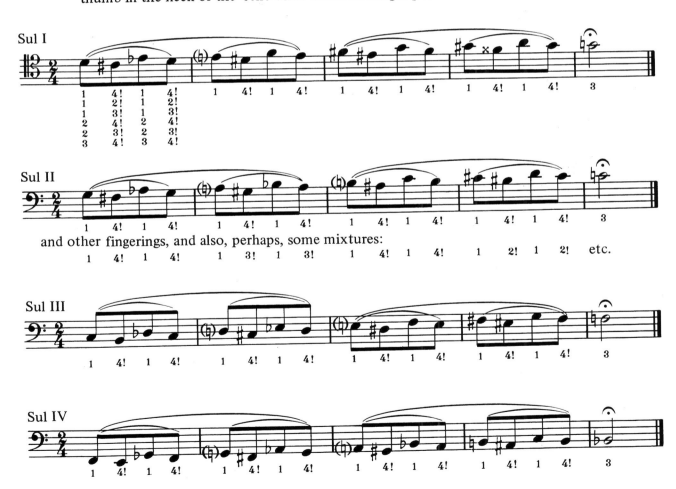

*Ex. 180*

Work this also with other shift-intervals, thus:

Sul I

Sul I

*Ex. 181*

As before, work the exercises with other fingerings, and on the other strings.

I have laboured this question of the downward shift in general and the downward shift of the fourth finger specifically because it is clear that much bad playing stems from a failure to come to terms with precisely this problem. No work on this cardinal point would be wasted.

When we come to the major and minor scales we find that we must execute cleanly downward shifts of now a tone, now a semitone. Let us take for example the scale of E major, on the A string, and practise it thus, utilizing the proficiency we have surely acquired from our labours:

Sul I

Sul I

*Ex. 182*

and A major on the D string:

Sul II

*Ex. 183*

and D major on the G string:

Sul III

*Ex. 184*

and G major on the C string:

Sul IV

*Ex. 185*

# *Shifting IV*

I feel that there may be material in this next section which may alienate some of my readers. I realize that in attempting to state factors which might better be left to such genius as we may individually dispose, I lay myself open to a charge of obfuscation. I feel that what I am talking about is merely the externalization of insights shared by all fine musicians, and that in these days of flirtation, if not yet solid relationship, between the Two Cultures, not as many players are as frightened by mathematical notions as were hitherto.

Perhaps I should here illuminate a sign reading:

NO SMOKING   FASTEN SEAT BELTS

Having cleaned up the downward shift we must now embark upon an enquiry into the upward shift. This can be functional or 'artistic', that is to say, a practical matter arising from our failure to deploy 187 fingers, or a means of emotional expression. I have intimated that in the case of the upward shift the distinction between functionality and artistry becomes a little blurred. It is a question of speed of movement, the vibrato, etc. It also depends upon the speed of the notes. A rapid arpeggio has minimum portamento and maximum clarity of articulation, approaching that of the piano. A slower upward movement of a phrase with the character of a cantilena may require a portamento such as would be executed by a fine singer. I am not here including in the discussion atonal music which demands special treatment.

There are, broadly speaking, two main categories of upward shift, and we must master both. The first I will christen 'K'. Here one slides up the first or second finger to a point below the top note, that note being played by the second, third, or fourth finger executing a percussion. A subsection of the K shift would embrace the case where top and bottom notes were played by the same finger, but another finger would execute the slide. This seemingly counter-productive procedure can make a beautiful effect.

**Examples of the K shift** (functional and/or expressive)

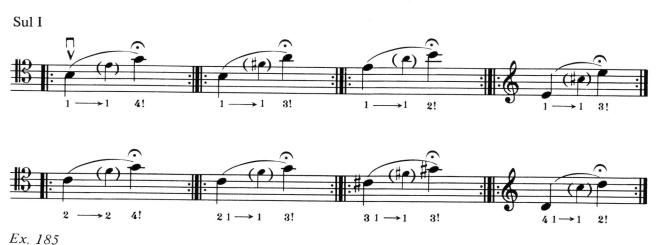

*Ex. 185*

From the artistic standpoint it is arguable that the K shift, with its nobility and relaxation, suits the nature of the 'cello better than the 'H' shift, to be presently described and which is sometimes thought to be a trifle 'slick'. Certainly the H shift is more fashionable nowadays, the K shift being considered rather *vieux jeu*.

I myself feel that if variety is as important as it surely must be, one must employ those means that are suitable to the given artistic situation. If an exciting upward portamento is required then there is no doubt that the K shift will not serve. However, we must be sparing in the use of the H shift, for nowadays there is a tendency to play in a style that can best be described as one of continuous excitement, the overall effect being one of stupefying boredom.

I have heard a record of Vivaldi's E minor sonata in which the player employs H shifts of the highest intensity, demonstrating a total insensitivity to the style and soul of the music. There is an absence of the required aristocratic bearing of the music; in its place is paraded a slick chromium-plated model. It is essential, as a basis for the cultivation of taste, to acquire the historical dimension, without, need it be said, being ensnared by the undoubted charms of pedantry.

The H shift is executed by sliding on the finger that is the same as the 'arrival finger'.

**Examples of the H shift** (functional and/or expressive)

*Ex. 186*

Although all four fingers can execute the H shift functionally, it is perhaps wiser to confine oneself to the second and third finger when the intention is predominantly expressive. Certainly it is more practical when one wishes to arrive with a fine expressive and intense vibrato on the top note, for these two fingers are more at the centre of the hand, and the natural oscillation is thus favoured.

With the K shift you will have noticed the little 'pivot' notes in brackets. To begin with, and even in performance sometimes, one should sound these notes. This helps to vivify the mechanism of the shift. I feel that it is important to choose these pivot notes with discrimination, for even when we allow them to 'atrophy' they colour the portamento with harmonic, and hence emotional, implications. Thus if we play:

*Ex. 187*

in an E major context or:

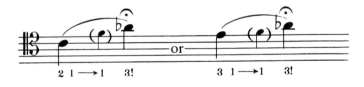

*Ex. 188*

in an F minor context, all is well. The interval is suitably 'seasoned', so to speak. But if we reverse these, playing the second example in an E major context and the first in an F minor one, a very disagreeable taste remains!

The portamento is a world in itself, and should be the object of the most devoted study. I will define it as 'a carrying of the thread of the music and associated feeling through the interval'. I am aware that the validity of this definition depends upon the acceptance of a certain delimited meaning of the word 'music' and that this would be challenged in some quarters. However, I am confident that most of us would know very exactly what would be connoted by 'the thread of the music'. Mozart called it the *filo*.

I have always felt that the interval is the really significant element in music, far more so than the note taken in isolation.

Each interval embodies a different emotional intensity and colour and this variable is multiplied by the proliferation of possible harmonic *décors*. When the

'Second Viennese School' produced their system of note-rows (composition by progressive choice-restriction), they might have done better to play their games with intervals as the basic building blocks of music.

Let us list some of the factors we should consider when making a portamento from one note to another:

1 Disparity or parity in the loudness levels of the two notes.
2 Variation of loudness during the portamento, whether between notes of equal or disparate loudness.
3 Variations in the vibrato, both in amplitude and frequency.
4 Rate of pitch-change.

These are musical variables. They are deployed and controlled by a set of technical variables:

1 Bow speed
2 Bow pressure
3 Point-of-contact
4 Vibrato
5 Rate of finger-movement

As these are all infinite variables and furthermore must be permuted the one with the other it will be seen that our only salvation is musico-technical intuition. We must integrate creatively this impossibly large number of variables. I have deliberately omitted a variable which in fact has a powerful bearing upon all this, namely 'Creative Intonation' (see p. 152) below.

Now, although I believe we are here in an area where to be merely scientific would be to be merely foolish, I must ask you to be patient whilst I deploy certain ideas about rate-of-change.

The simplest example of the rate-of-change is the linear one, that is to say that in equal amounts of time the variable varies by equal amounts.

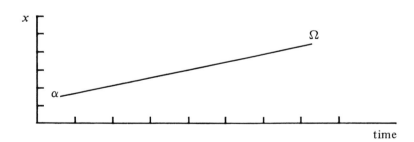

Thus, in the example above, if $x$ were loudness, each unit of elapsed time would entail an equal amount of increase in loudness. If $x$ were bow-speed, each unit of elapsed time would entail an equal amount of increase of the bow-speed.

Now, as loudness and bow-speed are separate variables we would already need a three-dimensional graph to represent an integration of these two and time! I have no idea how we would represent an integration of the large number of variables present in the playing of even a single note! But the method is valuable for elucidating discrete aspects.

Clearly, there is no reason why we must confine ourselves to the straight line, a linear relationship of the variables. With the straight line, the rate-of-change remained constant; but would it perhaps be more interesting if the rate-of-change itself changed? There is an infinity of curves that could take us from $\alpha$ to $\Omega$.

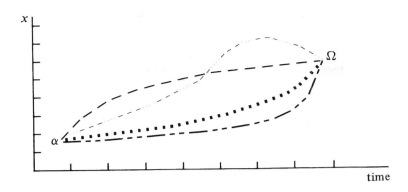

With – – – – – $x$ increases rapidly at first, the rate of increase progressively decreasing.

With –– – –– – $x$ increases gently at first, the rate of increase progressively increasing.

With • • • • • • • • • • • $x$ increases much in the fashion of – – – – – – but the rate of change is less dramatic.

With ⋯ – – – ⋯ – – – $x$ increases rapidly and reaches a maximum and then decreases to the value at $\Omega$.

Don't forget that $x$ can represent any of our variables, bow-speed, loudness, point-of-contact change, vibrato frequency, vibrato amplitude, rate of pitch-change, and so forth.

Dare I say that another factor that will have to be incorporated is the syllabic diminuendo (see vol. 1, p. 90)? Perhaps I am already in danger of straining your tolerance to breaking point!

Now I have had two motives in leading you through this jungle, one general and the other specific. Firstly I wish you, as an aspirant to conscious artistry, to be thinking about the factors involved in a general sense. That is to say that I wish you to know what the situation is, what the possibilities, and thus to permit you to choose intelligently. Secondly I want to persuade you to the ideas I shall now propound so that the choice may be artistically fruitful and creative.

Newton tells us that the force equals the mass multiplied by the acceleration – $P = mf$, where P is the force, m the mass and f the acceleration. I feel that there is an aesthetic analogy to this mechanical law. Motion and emotion are words that are semantically linked. There can be no such thing as a static emotion. I believe this to be intuitively understood by all fine players and indeed composers, and even by painters! One can see its operation in both the tactics and strategy of the Marx Brothers' films. Bad art and bad philosophy are always linear!

If you wish to bore your audience, keep P steady, that is, keep the rate-of-change steady. Note however that boredom, in smallish doses, has its part to play in 'setting off' the nodal moments making a dramatic point.

If you wish to increase P, increase f, that is, *increase the rate of increase*.

Let us take a practical example. Let us look at our old friend the crescendo. The linear crescendo will merely apply a steady force upon the audience. The audience, by the way, is represented in the equation by m – the mass to be moved! Of course, some audiences are denser than others . . . For the force upon the audience to increase in a crescendo the loudness must increase logarithmically, geometrically if you will. In equal amounts of time the rate of increase in loudness increases. Thus:

Thus:

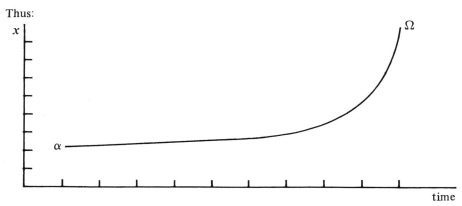

You have been very patient. May I take another step? Even in our new diagram we have but achieved a steadily, that is linearly(!), increasing P. I suggest that for an exciting logarithmic curve for P we must in fact *progressively increase the rate at which the rate of increase in loudness increases*. Calm yourself! That is the final onion-skin and, I trust, not the last straw. The phrase is worth reading several times, and might conceivably be set to music!

Returning to the immediate question of the upward slide, it will surely be conceded that intuition must be granted plenary powers, even if that intuition has been intuitive enough to incorporate and integrate my ideas!

Let me say immediately that it would be a solecism to replicate exactly the performance of two consecutive and similar musical elements. Casals was always very stringent about this. Thus, in the following, let us, for example, execute the leap of the sixth as a K shift, and following this the leap of the fifth in the second bar as an H shift.

*Ex. 189*

This ploy, for all its validity, is a trifle naive. Experiment with a reversal: permute all the possibilities, not forgetting bowing variants. Alternatively start the phrase with a down-bow or an up-bow. Integrate all the possibilities of linear and logarithmic crescendi and diminuendi. Integrate the syllabic diminuendo (see vol. 1, p. 90). One could indeed profitably spend hours upon this one phrase.

The following will be found helpful:

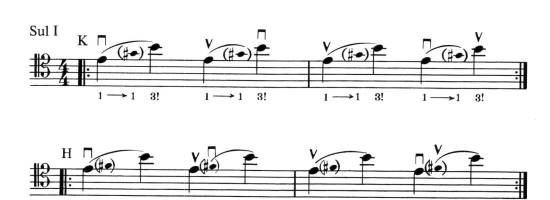

Sul II

Sul III

Sul IV

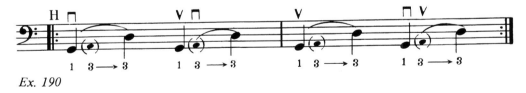

*Ex. 190*

Now work with other intervals; also starting on other notes. With the K shift take a pivot-note one minor third lower than the top note when using 1 3, one tone when using 1 2, unless the demands of harmonic 'seasoning' (p. 115) indicate otherwise.

Before we come on to the work-out, let us look at the case where we change bow during the slide, perhaps half-way, perhaps not. This occurs in Saint-Saëns' *Le Cygne*, and indeed quite frequently. It should not be attempted by players with bad coordination.

*Ex. 191*

119

If done with taste, a deliciously 'floating' feeling can be brought about. Experiment with bowing reversals, and various dynamic patterns. Throw the clay onto the wheel and try it this way and that.

# *Portamento Work-out*

**(Work-out of portamento slides on the same string deploying all the intervals enclosed by an octave.)**

Use the procedures previously described. Use both K and H shifts, alternately or alternatively, in varying permutations. Occasionally vary the bowing, but always to a plan. Practise each group retrogradely. At first keep the dynamic level unvarying. Later introduce variations, but, again, always to a set plan. This is not the place for haphazard fantasy. The whole 'ladder' could be on a crescendo or a diminuendo with the two-note groups themselves level, or on a crescendo or diminuendo. Even this could be further subdivided:

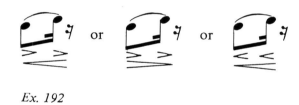

*Ex. 192*

Practise rather slowly at first. Practise occasionally, but certainly not always, with the metronome.

It is worthwhile to point out that, as in the case of broken octaves on the piano, there are 'hidden' intervals involved. I refer to the interval between the second and third notes, the fourth and fifth, and so on. Thus with the minor thirds rising by semitones this hidden interval is a tone. With fifths, similarly, the interval is an augmented fourth.

Why should one engage oneself in all this unmusical drudgery? I believe it to be important that one builds up an ever more vivid mental and tactile image of the 'lattice', *away* from the musical context. A certain neutrality is essential, as is a confidence in the predictability and replicability of the correct technical gestures. This technique is then available for artistic application.

Continue the patterns up to the harmonic on the quarter string point, or some other convenient note.

All the intervals mentioned are equitemperamental. If you are irritated with this, I am encouraged to hope that you will be sympathetic to the section on Creative Intonation (p. 152, below). For someone sensitive to the integrity of keys it is difficult even to write down the patterns which follow.

Portamento exercise 1
*Minor thirds rising by semitones* (chromatic)
*Hidden interval = a tone*

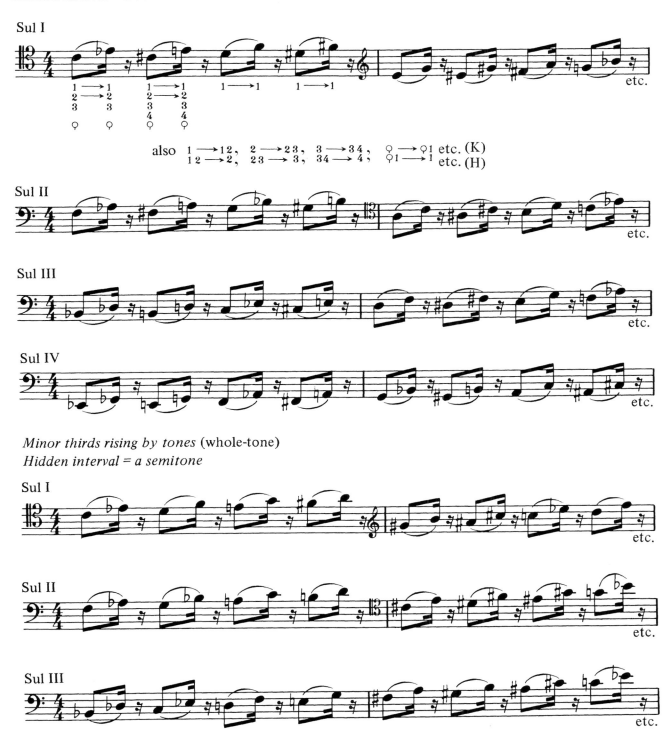

*The Left Hand*

*Major thirds rising by semitones* (chromatic)
*Hidden interval = a minor third*

Sul I

Sul II

Sul III

Sul IV

*Major thirds rising by tones* (whole-tone)
*Hidden interval = a tone*

Sul I

Sul II

Sul III

Sul IV

*Fourths rising by semitones* (chromatic)
*Hidden interval = a major third*

Sul I

Sul II

Sul III

Sul IV

*Fourths rising by tones* (whole-tone)
*Hidden interval = a minor third*

Sul I

Sul II

Sul III

Sul IV

*Augmented fourths/diminished fifths rising by semitones* (chromatic)
*Hidden interval = fourth*

Sul I

Sul II

Sul III

Sul IV

*Augmented fourths/diminished fifths rising by tones* (whole-tone)
*Hidden interval = major third*

Sul I

Sul II

Sul III

Sul IV

*Fifths rising by semitones* (chromatic)
*Hidden interval = augmented fourth (tritone)*

*Fifths rising by tones* (whole-tone)
*Hidden interval = fourth*

125

*Minor sixths rising by semitones* (chromatic)
*Hidden interval = fifth*

*Minor sixths rising by tones* (whole-tone)
*Hidden interval = augmented fourth (tritone)*

*Major sixths rising by semitones* (chromatic)
*Hidden interval = minor sixth*

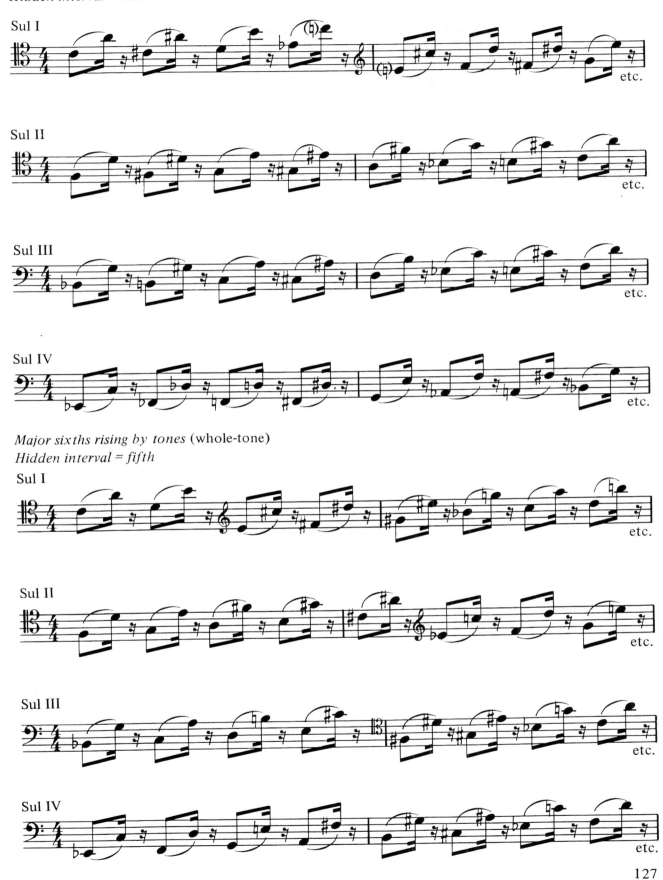

*Major sixths rising by tones* (whole-tone)
*Hidden interval = fifth*

*Minor sevenths rising by semitones* (chromatic)
*Hidden interval = major sixth*
Sul I

Sul II

Sul III

Sul IV

*Major sevenths rising by tones* (whole-tone)
*Hidden interval = minor sixth*
Sul I

Sul II

Sul III

Sul IV

*Major sevenths rising by semitones* (chromatic)
*Hidden interval = minor seventh*

*Major sevenths rising by tones* (whole-tone)
*Hidden interval = major seventh*

*Octaves rising by semitones* (chromatic)
*Hidden interval = major seventh*

*Octaves rising by tones* (whole-tone)
*Hidden interval = minor seventh*

*Ex. 193*

## Portamento Work-out

Practice in controlling the portamento, tone, intonation, vibrato, and associated factors is so important that I propose the following supplementary exercises. Take any note a tenth or so above the open string and work your way through the intervals in the manner following:

Portamento exercise 2
(The same finger throughout)

* if playing in octaves (p. 140) begin the retrogression here.

**Sul III**

**Sul IV**

*Ex. 194*

Portamento exercise 3
Remember that the same interval up and down does not imply an equal distance
along the strings.

Sul I

and retrogradely.

Sul II

and retrogradely.

Sul III

and retrogradely.

Sul IV

*Ex. 195*

and retrogradely.

The creative student will explore the patterns starting on many different notes.

The format I have chosen in the two preceding studies is the least taxing. It would be profitable, as one's expertise advances, to practise the following:

In Ex. 193:

*Ex. 196*

In Ex. 195:

*Ex. 197*

When you are self-programming, so to speak, make sure that your inner mental voice names each new note, and that your inner mental ear hears each new note, a fraction of a second before you sound it. Otherwise the work will be largely wasted. Reflect that practising the 'cello is vastly different from painting a battleship. At the end of the shift you can look at the battleship and see how much you have painted. There is visible evidence of your labours. With 'cello practice all that remains is a clearer mental picture and a reinforcement of the hierarchically organized links between the nerves, both instructing and assessing, the muscles and the computer. Thus most practice is mental practice.

Further practice, with piano accompaniment, may be pursued in my *Patinages* (Cambridge University Press, 1982).

## The 'false' portamento

It is sometimes inconvenient to take the larger intervals on the same string. *Per contra*, it is occasionally good tactics to change strings during a theme. If this interval is taken 'cold' there may be a certain musical shock — a dislocation of the continuity or logic of the theme. When I spoke of 'tactics' I was primarily thinking about cheironomic choreography, but musically and emotionally it sometimes pays to jump into a different 'gear' so to speak, a quantum leap of the theme! Thus a virtue can be made out of necessity and tactics necessitate this virtue!

I do not apologize for analysing all these procedures thus clinically, but I hope it is clearly understood that nothing will avail unless the techniques are deployed with intuition and imagination.

Let us remind ourselves of the material in 'Shifting IV' descriptive of the many variables available to us. Now the 'false' portamento occurs when we take the two notes to be connected on two different and usually adjacent strings and imitate the effect of the true portamento by sliding either one or both fingers. Of course the real effect is discontinuous, but with careful shading with the bow an illusion of continuity can be obtained.

There are three categories: (i) when the slide is exclusively on the lower finger (from the lower note; quasi-'K'), (ii) when the slide is exclusively on the higher finger (to the higher note; quasi-'H'), and (iii) when both (i) and (ii) are present.

(i) (quasi-K)

*Ex. 198*

As we have seen before the 'pivot' or 'ghost' note, call it what you will, 'seasons' the flavour of the portamento, and hence must be chosen with knowledge and intuition. Naturally this choice influences the overall fingering.

(ii) (quasi-H)

*Ex. 199*

With the third category, a mixture of (i) and (ii), much cunning is required in the blending of the various acceleration patterns of bow pressure and speed, as discussed in 'Shifting IV'.

(iii)

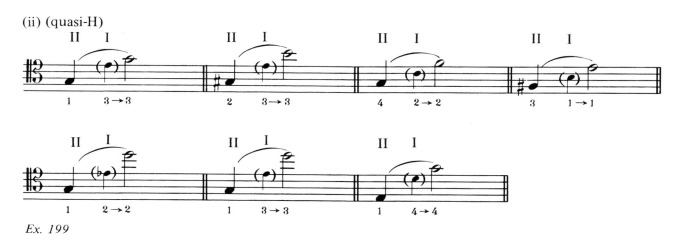

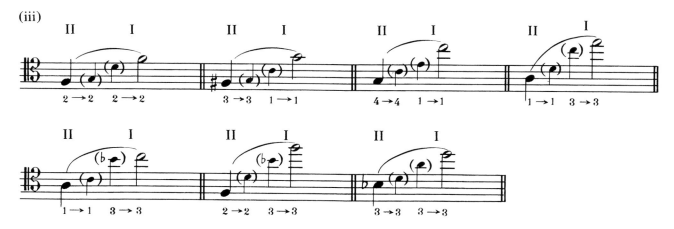

*Ex. 200*

As before, it is important to work these exercises on down-bows and up-bows, and also with separate bows on each note. Always begin to approach closely the string upon which is located the second note as you complete the bow-stroke of the first, in other words, streamline the bowing gestures.

The downwards false portamento is perhaps a rare bird, but similar principles apply.

(i) (Of limited value, to be executed with discrimination)

(ii) (Imparting an air of resignation)

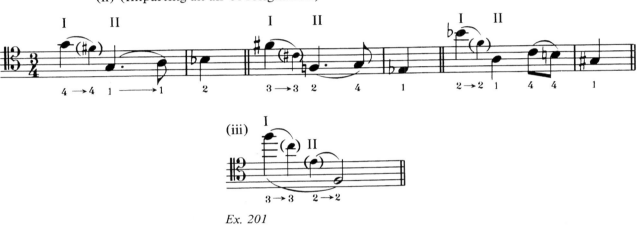

(iii)

*Ex. 201*

# The 'Six-fingered' hand

It is said that Samuel Dushkin, entrusted with the first performance of the violin concerto of Stravinsky, came to the composer complaining that the work needed six fingers. The story has it that Stravinsky's response was – 'I'll wait!'

Often a phrase lies awkwardly in that it takes more than the handful of fingers to encompass it. Composers who are predominantly keyboard-biassed tend to think in five-finger handfuls, whereas string-biassed composers think rather in four-finger handfuls.

To avoid clumsy and frequent shifting one can often take two adjacent notes a semitone apart *with the same finger*. Most phrases have a semitone somewhere.

Clearly, if one is going to make rapid movements with the left hand and forearm, the body-use must be good: if one is in effect trying to shift part of one's body-weight with the arm, things are not going to have a happy outcome. Experience the support (buttocks and feet), allow spine-lengthening (permitting natural breathing), and let the shoulders lie low. Give yourself the luxury of a free head-spine joint (the most important and the most elusive of all).

**Exercises**

*Ex. 202*

Zig-zags (p. 94 above) will also be found relevant and also Popper Opus 76 (*Preparatory Studies for the High School*) no. 7.

# Cheironomic Choreography

In the early stages players are encouraged to hold down the fingers in the positions. This practice doubtless has a certain utility as an *aide-mémoire*. Unfortunately, early teaching becomes a vivid part of our personal history and takes on a dispro-

138

portionate numinosity. If this practice links up with a tendency towards the ocnophilia described by Dr Michael Balint,* an essential development may never take place.

I am sure you have heard of Ivan Ivanovitch, the eccentric 'cellist, who spends his life always playing the same note. After many years his patient wife questioned him about it. 'Natasha, my love, you are stupid — all the other 'cellists are looking for the place, I've found it!'

Well, if nothing else, he is living in the present! So few of us do. We are anxious about the past and the future, vitiating our experience of present reality.

The 'positions' should progressively be organized into a mental map of the 'cello, a map of great subtlety when we integrate the ideas about creative intonation. It will have imaginary contours delineating imaginary concavities and convexities associated with the hand shapes that 'form' the triads and phrases. One may then dispense with the paralysing practice of clamping the fingers in each position, and dedicate each note to Ivan Ivanovitch! Consider:

*Ex. 203*

One's impulse is to say 'Ah! First position!' Very well, but supposing the music is marked *adagio*? There is plenty of time to enjoy the B, with a clear beginning due to kinetic touch and a vibrato, with the other fingers helpfully clustering around the first. At a certain moment the fourth finger will begin its kinetic preparation, allied to an opening-out of the hand and a subtle readjustment of the first finger. For a wee moment the hand will indeed be 'in first position' before clustering around an established fourth finger singing D expressively in the manner previously displayed by the first. If the tempo-marking were *andantino* the principles of cheironomic choreography** still apply. If the tempo were *presto*, then of course we would have to think again. The most economical movements would be sought. 'Time and Motion' study would come to our aid (but beware, its inventor went mad).

A subtle but important point: it is vital to develop the action and mutual independence of the fingers with an *uninvolved* hand, a hand that is not misused to 'help' a weak finger — usually the fourth. Having ensured this, one can then follow and reinforce the finger-action with movements of the hand.

I have often seen a dramatic breakthrough in fluency and expressiveness when a student has understood this emancipated use of the left hand.

It is important to develop smoothness of hand-movement between non-contiguous 'positions', especially when separated by a string change. Consider:

---

* See volume 1, Prelude, p. 4 and bibliography, p. 13.
** I coined this term lightly as it enables me to codify the alliteration as $ch^2$.

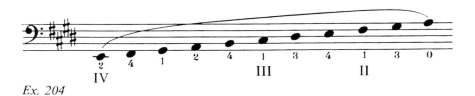

*Ex. 204*

When left-hand 4 has been established on F♯, 1 and 2 can begin to move upwards 'through' the hand. As B is approached, the first finger begins to point *back* towards C♯ on the G string. The bow approaches the correct angle for the G string ('streamlining') and as C♯ is established, the left hand clusters around the first finger. As E is reached, the first finger points back to F♯ on the D string. Each note is dedicated to Ivan Ivanovitch, and the finger playing it takes the weight of the hand and forearm in due proportion, singing with a free vibrato.

# Octaves

We have already done some work in the thumb-positions, navigating by means of the movable grids embodying the idea of the two tetrachords, one on each of two adjacent strings.

One of the diagonals of the grid is the octave, and thus any work that may bring our octave playing to a high quality will also bring a twofold benefit: our playing in the thumb-positions will improve generally, and also we will master in principle all those octave passages to be found in the concerto literature.

A cursory glance at the hand suggests that whereas the fingers clearly have three phalanges the thumb has only two. Now we know that body-use tends to follow the mental model whether that model is correct or incorrect. Many players use their thumb precisely in a way that assumes that there are indeed only two phalanges.

Have another look!

Better still, examine an X-ray photograph of the hand. Is it not extraordinary how much we know about the world outside ourselves, and how little of the very stuff of our own beings?

I have earlier shown you how to lay the thumb in relation to one and two strings (p. 60). A little work on the third finger in relation to the thumb in the exercise called 'Snakes' (p. 12) will strengthen and 'plasticize' the muscular arch employed in octave playing.*

I feel that the secret lies in the movement of the thumb. If the thumb is in tune and the muscular arch between it and the third finger is strong and plastic, then it is a relatively simple matter to place the third finger also in tune. So, get into the habit of playing tunes with the thumb only. At first choose tunes that do not have large intervals: I suggest the 'Harry Lime' theme from the film *The Third Man* to begin with, as it proceeds mainly by semitones. *God Save the Queen* might form the next step. The *ne plus ultra* would, I suppose, be the waltz from *Der*

* My *Six Resilience Studies* (Cambridge University Press, 1982) will be found valuable.

*Rosenkavalier*! Sometimes let the third finger move on its 'octave-place' without the note being sounded by the bow.

The following exercises are usually found to be helpful. Sometimes reverse the bowing. Sometimes use the pattern: ♪ ♪ ♩ ♩ | ♪ ♪ ♩ ♩ :‖. Always bear in mind the cardinal rule that the thumb moves a greater distance than does the third finger, whether ascending or descending. Rest a little between each exercise, or play some completely different material.

Octaves 1 (i)

Octaves 2 (i)

Octaves 1 (ii)

Octaves 2 (ii)

*Ex. 205*

I have provided two transpositions of Octaves 1 and Octaves 2 because I know we are all frail and lazy. However, may I beg you not to stop there, but to proceed higher and also to work pegwards. Also, carry the work on to the other pairs of strings.

Having acquired some competence in the foregoing material, the way forward might well be via the broken octaves in Grützmacher's *Daily Exercises* (Schirmer edn, 1909, 1937), and via the Stutschewsky *Studien* (Schott edn 1371) vol. 1, p. 41.

Mindful that any technical expertise must be well-enough established to bear the stress of the emotion inherent in musical performance, practise Popper Opus

76 no. 5 and Opus 73 no. 13. It is essential that when one comes to the concertos the technical groundwork has long before been done.

Here are some exercises based upon an idea borrowed from Clara Schumann. Notice how important a balanced body-use is, especially in relation to the larger shifts. As before, rest between each exercise.

*Ex. 206*

One disadvantage of the foregoing exercises is that the movements are either symmetrical or follow linearly incremental changes, whereas real music pursues its course through a multiplicity of intervals following an emotional/imaginative logic, with the exception, of course, of twentieth-century 'amusic'. Thus I think we must exercise in the diatonic modes. Be conscious of the overt intervals (major and minor thirds), and also the hidden intervals as described in 'Shifting IV'.

Octaves 4

*Ex. 207*

Play this also in other keys.

Sometimes we use what are called 'fingered octaves'. When we want to avoid any hint of a slide between the notes this technique becomes essential.

*Ex. 208*

Clearly we can only employ these means in the 'upper' half of the instrument. It is usually found that the interval of a semitone is more uncomfortable than that of the tone.

*Ex. 209*

At the higher pitches we can quite comfortably encompass the interval of a minor third. Refer to Stutschewsky's studies p. 43. I personally prefer the fingering $\frac{3\ 4}{\varphi\ 1}$ to $\frac{2\ 3}{\varphi\ 1}$

I will give two examples of the use of fingered octaves to clean up passages that would by another technique be performed indistinctly. The first comes from the last movement of Haydn's D major concerto:

*Ex. 210*

Here is another example, from the Finale of the *Rococo Variations* by Tchaikovsky:

*Ex. 211*

The bowing shown above is, of course, only one pattern among many possible ones. See also *Six Resilience Studies*, Cambridge University Press, 1982.

It would clearly be advantageous to practise octaves in portamento, in the manner suggested in the Portamento Work-out (p. 120).

*Ex. 212*

and, as at p. 131:

*Ex. 213*

working through *all intervals*, and with all pairs of strings.

Clearly one should also practise every other interval in these permutations: sevenths in octave leaps, in sevenths, in sixths, etc. I do not apologize that this might well keep the student out of mischief for many a month!

*Ex. 219*

As with thirds, relief is sometimes to be had via the occasional open string, but, in general, 'running' sixths are liable to be awkward. The following is from Brahms' clarinet trio:

*Ex. 220*

One little bonus can be had towards the end of Bach's third solo prelude, where we find a trill in sixths. Matters become simpler if we recall the rule that with the trill on a tone the interval must be enlarged. Fortunately in this case it is only the lower notes that trill on the tone interval, providing us with an alternation of major and minor sixths. Note that the B of the first sixth is *not* a perfect fifth above the E of the second.

*Ex. 221*

There is a passage in mixed sixths in Saint-Saëns' A minor concerto which may be fingered as follows.

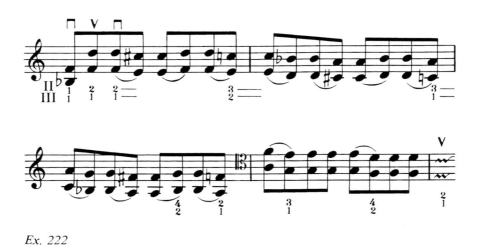

*Ex. 222*

A competence in sliding accurately through semitone displacements is the prerequisite for performance of the first movement of Dvořák's B minor concerto. A very finely attuned ear is essential if one is to deploy the *unequal* semitones (see the section on Creative Intonation which follows).

# Creative Intonation

I intend the phrase 'Creative Intonation' to embrace three conceptual areas: (i) a mental attitude that is more positive and cybernetically realistic than that commonly held, (ii) 'expressive intonation', a phrase already current and meaning 'the modification of intonation for empirical, subjective and essentially artistic reasons', and (iii) the musical insights codified in the multiplicity of scales, modes and temperaments from the earliest times until now.

I remember teaching a boy at the Yehudi Menuhin School and arriving at the point where the question of contextual and sensitive intonation had become timely. The boy was distressed. 'All my life' — he was eight — 'I've been trying to play in tune, and now you come along and say that I must play out of tune!' Fortunately this *crise pédagogique* was resolved and the boy progressed.

Two questions:

1 Upon what do you base your intonational scheme?
2 Why did you choose to play an instrument that offers *infinite* variability of pitch?

I suppose that no culture may enjoy periods of great flowering unless there is at the time a central schema, and music is no exception. The inventions of the equally-tempered scale and its acolyte the piano are central facts in the music of the last two-and-a-half centuries, and a great literature has arisen. Indeed without the simplistic equal temperament and the piano the history of western music would have been radically different, probably impoverished. Bach, Handel, Mozart, Beethoven, Brahms, Rachmaninov, Stravinsky, Poulenc, Britten and Bartók were all keyboard virtuosi and thought 'keyboard'.

However there is a negative side to this need for mental structures, as Erich Fromm has pointed out,* and many of the horrors of our century stem immediately from this cause. Note that of the composers cited those innocent of the twentieth century were also string players, and were thus in touch with the *infinite* variables associated with unmediated nature (nature raw rather than 'cut-and-dried'). I hope I have shown clearly in the Prelude that defences against reality belong to an early or regressed phase of development. We all need our defences, but there must be a balance, and I think the great composers of the eighteenth and nineteenth century seem to have achieved this.

I will spare you immersion in a sea of theories about scales and temperaments. We are looking for that which is found to be effective, by experiment and reality-testing. I do however feel that you might like to read the relevant chapters in the books by Alexander Wood or Sir James Jeans and make the acquaintance of such fauna as hemitones, limmas and commas.

The main thing is to hold on to the simple ratios, not in genuflection to any idea of Cosmic Truth but because of the principle of *reinforcement*. If we base our intonation on the simple ratios, the partial and sympathetic vibrations of the strings will be in harmony and reinforce one another.

I am not sure whether I am prepared to accept the theory that a 'cello habitually played in natural intonation 'opens up' and progressively develops a more beautiful tone, but wood is certainly a strange material. The speed of sound in the winter growth and the summer growth differs widely. The weather continually affects its

* Erich Fromm, *The Fear of Freedom*, Routledge, 1942, and *Anatomy of Human Destructiveness*, Jonathan Cape, 1974.

mechanical properties. The effect of rapid alternations of stress on the molecular organization of materials is only slowly being understood. Thus the theory is not as fanciful as it might at first sight appear. I would certainly advise any 'cellist convinced of his strong and sound intuition to follow that intuition confidently. Certain it is that some 'cellists can make the most beautiful 'cellos sound dreadful and others can make the veriest tea-crate sing!

I return then to the first of the questions I put to you. If your idea of scales and intonation is based on the tuning of the piano you are trafficking in a corruption, to put it dramatically! This corruption was partially endorsed by J.S. Bach, and wholly endorsed by his son C.P.E. Bach, but I do not think that by virtue of this exalted name it should be granted critical immunity. The organs Bach played were not tuned equitemperamentally and we know that the pitch of a clavichord note varies considerably with the touch. Clearly we do not know what intonation he used when playing the violin or viola. One doubts whether a music such as Bach's, so dependent upon, and lovingly exploitative of, key identities and modulations, would welcome vitiation of either from egalitarian motivation.

The tuning of the piano has to be a compromise. Even the fifth, tuned in equal temperament, has to be flat, and here do not forget what Helmholtz tells us, that the maximum dissonance occurs closest to the consonance, because the frequency of the beats increases. A 'near' fifth is more dissonant than an augmented fourth, the dreaded tritone! Think of all those partials fighting one another with the equitemperamental fifth! However, the greatest interval distortion on the piano occurs with the major third. Delezenne made measurements of Joachim's intonation and found that his major third was significantly higher than that to be expected from equal temperament. In other words it was closer to the natural third.

It appears to me that this question of the third is a crucial one, for it is the 'characterizing' interval determining whether the scale is major or minor. Thus it is vital in the major tetrachord to make a large major third out of two large tones and accept a small semitone between the third and fourth degree of the scale. Whether the connecting tone be 'disjunct' or no, the complete scale is then achieved by piling a similarly constructed tetrachord upon the first. There can then be logical modulation to the dominant, the 'aspiration of music' as Ansermet has said, because the second tetrachord of the tonic key becomes the first tetrachord of its dominant. Moreover, the leading note of the tonic, leading a double life, becomes the mediant of the dominant. What marvellous things Bach does with this fact.

The lower tetrachord of the minor scale is constructed from a large tone, a small semitone, making, together, a small minor third, and another tone. What marvels Elgar makes possible with the tension of the sharp F♯, and the flat mediant G in E minor. The upper minor tetrachord of course varies as to whether it is of the harmonic or melodic form. In the harmonic form the sixth should be flatter than that of equal temperament, the seventh sharper. In the melodic form ascending, the situation is the same as that for a major tetrachord, in descent a major tetrachord in reverse, so to speak, two large tones and a small semitone.

It has been said that the intonation of an ascending major scale should differ from that of the same scale descending. Ascending, we naturally emphasize the aspiring leaps, descending we characterize the sense of relaxation, or resigned sadness.

You will notice that I have used imprecise terms. I have done this deliberately for two reasons: (i) the whole matter must be one of testing and refinement, and (ii) there is the speed factor of the various stimuli, which will be discussed presently.

I am sure that the idea of the 'magnetization' of notes, attracting or repelling one another, is of great value. The major third and seventh are pulled upward by their strong neighbours. The minor third is pulled down by the second.

Now I am fully aware that all the foregoing has been a gross simplification, and doubtless insulting to the more sensitive of my readers. Creative intonation is, after all, an art in its own right. Menuhin, when in an elevated spiritual rapture, often plays a sharpened fifth, always convincing. However I believe that if only the simple rules were more widely followed, both performers and listeners would benefit.

I am told that Casals was once overheard carefully practising the interval of a tone, from the open string to the first finger. Clearly this is more difficult than the tone made between two fingers, but the point is that Casals felt the need to *create* that interval anew every day.

And so we come to the concept of Creative Intonation. We have seen (p. 6 above, and in the Prelude, vol. 1) how sterile, from the cybernetic point of view, 'perfectionism' is, if indeed the word is not actually meaningless. '*Ex perfecto nihil fit*' said the old masters. It is unsound to 'match' one's intonation to a pattern (especially an equitemperamental one), and utterly negative. How often have I noticed that perfectionist pupils following a matching intonational scheme have gross functional distortions with the associated muscular tensions. Re-educating the functioning must surely be inappropriate without a radical re-adjustment of the psychosomatic attitude. Let us rather imagine a beautiful interval with all its colour and tension, and associated conformation of the hand, and carry this clear image positively into the actual creation of a musical event. These intervals and hand positions will then be organized meaningfully into a sequence within the encompassing scales, arpeggios and chords.

I believe this to be a radical change of viewpoint.

Small adjustments will be made continually within the 'envelope' of the scalic rules and according to artistic intuition. This contextual shaping of the intonation is part of the fascination of string-playing, analogous to the pleasure of shaping clay on the wheel.

Unfortunately we must occasionally deny ourselves these luxuries. For example, when we have to play a theme in unison with the piano (e.g. Beethoven Opus 69 bars 16-17) we must accept the yoke and align our intonation with its equitemperance, in this instance denying ourselves that delicious sharp D♯ leading us into E major.

However, I am bound to say that I have heard Szigeti 'get away' with a disparity of intonation in an analogous context. Listen to his marvellous performance of Beethoven's Kreutzer sonata with Bartók, recorded in America during the Second World War.

This takes us into deep water, for the *subjective* impression of pitch, our *experience* of pitch, is influenced by many factors; loudness, sharpness of wave-front and timbre. Also, the level of the pitch of the note is itself a factor. Each of us has a mental frequency-spectrum and can discriminate pitch and timbre-differences differentially, related to the nearness or otherwise of the note to the preferred areas of that spectrum. Men and women differ in this consciousness, the disparity being doubtless related to the different tessiturae of their voices. Of course men at least have a mental image of the soprano voice before the break at puberty, whereas most women have not had the analogous experience. Women musicians have told me that they have noted a correlation between a variability in pitch-discrimination and their physical phases. This factor also has an effect, it seems, on the strength of the absolute pitch 'image' in those blessed or cursed with this ability.

I was forcibly made aware of the effect of timbre upon the subjective experience of pitch when I listened to two tape recordings taken from a concerto broadcast that I had given not long before. One recording was a good 'high-fidelity' one, the other 'low-fidelity', with attentuation of the upper frequencies which dramatically altered the timbre. A certain passage in the soprano register of the 'cello contained an F♯ which I remembered as having played 'in tune'; that is, I remembered having consciously chosen the intonation of that note in its context, and furthermore that I actualized my intention. This was confirmed upon listening to the good recording, but on the bad recording *this one note* sounded flat! Just one note! I recall that it was a melodic-summit note. Of course you have only my word for it, and the whole thing is very subjective, but I suggest that something very peculiar is happening here. Perhaps there is here a whole area of knowledge as yet unexplored, but which the fine player bestrides unerringly with his sound intuition.

Another case where we may have to abandon creative intonation is that of the diminished arpeggio (a pile of equitemperamental minor thirds). In this we must not use as our building unit the true minor third (6:5) as this would bring us out at the wrong place!

A third case would be that of the true chromatic scale; unless we use equitemperamental semitones we will arrive in a very weird situation!

However, in seeking to give you examples of these last two categories my thoughts turned to the Saint-Saëns A minor concerto, and I found that the examples I had in mind proved the *opposite*! If you look at bar 14 of this work, you will find that the solo 'cellist plays a descending diminished arpeggio, a cascade of equitemperamental minor thirds, one would think. Ah! but look more closely. Is there not a very strong sense of impending E major in the air? Does this not imply that the D♯s should assume the rôle of leading notes and thus be sharpened? An interesting point here concerns the final D♯ (bar 15). If we sharpen it, will it clash with the woodwind chord? The only difficulty might arise from the bassoon D♯, but it is an octave higher, and the disparity of pitch and timbre, not to speak of vibrato, should take care of things. As always we have to steer through conflicting considerations and must try to establish the correct priorities. In this case the integrity of the solo line is paramount.

Turning to bars 53 and 54 of the same work we see what appears to be a long egalitarian chromatic scale. But, surely the whole two bars are coloured by the impending A minor, and it is this that gives them their *raison d'être*. Thus the C♯s must be sharpened, the Cs flattened and, I would say, the D♯s sharpened. *Thus the semitones are decidedly not of equal size.*

Let us now turn our attention to the B minor concerto, Opus 104, of Dvořák. Look at bars 187 and 188 of the last movement, twenty-one bars after no. 5. Woven into the chromatic scale is surely the colour of a dominant seventh chord seeking its consummation in a D major chord, finally achieved at no. 6. The solution here is temporarily to expunge all the notes alien to the A major scale, to sharpen the C♯s and G♯s, and then to reintroduce the aliens, the A♯s, B♯s, D♯s and E♯s, as weak passing notes *magnetized* upward by the pull of the A major notes.

There is another factor to be taken into account and I call it 'the Coefficient of Casals'. We have agreed, I trust, that equal temperament will not satisfy us, and we have examined some of the determinants of what I have called Creative Intonation. Now this added factor is that the sharpening, flattening and magnetization of notes must also be related to the *tempo* of the music, usually in the sense that the modifications increase in amount as the tempo increases. Thus, again in the last movement of Dvořák's concerto, immediately after our 'seasoned' chromatic scale come two bars of semitone trill. Now it is a matter of experience, in both senses of the word, that a better focussing of the semitone trill is given if the interval used is less than a semitone, considerably less, the amount of such modification being related to the speed of the trill. Of course, this poses quite a problem when we play high up in the soprano register of the 'cello. The solution is to lay the second finger along the side of the first finger in such a way that when we execute a very rapid vibrato of the latter the second finger is brought down upon the string with every bridgeward oscillation. I would not advise this procedure in this case, but it would certainly be suitable in the slow movement, six bars from the end.

The two succeeding bars of the concerto (last movement, bars 191 and 192) will serve as a prototype of the case where there is a 'polarization' around one note, in this case an A. Here the B♭ and the G♯ must be drawn inwards toward the A, *the amount of this modification increasing with increasing speed.*

Play the passage and also this close cousin to it:

*Ex. 223*

at various speeds and observe for yourself the operation of this law. Try also:

(Elgar concerto)

*Ex. 224*

(Beethoven Opus 69)

*Ex. 225*

and

(Tchaikovsky *Rococo Variations*)

*Ex. 226*

Play these passages at all pitches on the instrument and see how the effect alters also with pitch!

A little later, again in the last movement of the Dvořák concerto, we come to the trill of a whole tone, (bar 197, seven bars before no. 6). Again it is a matter of experience, commonly assented to, that to focus the character of this trill, we must make the interval considerably *more* than a tone. Again, experiment. Satisfy yourself that the idea is a sound one.

Quite often in eighteenth-century majestic slow movements we want to make a trill of a whole tone which starts slowly and then speeds up. Here, of course the interval must increase as the speed of the trill increases.

How does this speed-related pitch-modification affect the major scale? I have said before that it is the mediant that is the 'characterizing' note, therefore it would be logical to increase the sharpening with increasing speed. Play:

*Ex. 227*

at varying speeds, experimenting with the intonation of the mediant and the leading note, both in this case taken by the second finger. Then experiment with bar 61 of the last movement of Beethoven's Opus 69.

Taking bars 40 and 41 of the same movement, we might want to enlarge the size of the major third 'envelope', because of the speed. It is a help to 'roll' the hand, pivoting on the second finger. Certainly in bar 42 the D♯ and the A♯ must be sharpened the more decisively to wrench the listening brain out of E major and into B major.

Allow me to interpose a thought. Let us realize that as we throw the fingers out in a rapid sequence centrifugal force will tend to make them land on the sharp side of the target, increasingly so as the speed increases. Whether this effect is or is not congruent with the required sharpening is a question that can only be resolved by experiment.

As far as I know, no one has offered any explanation of all these curious phenomena on the frontier between objectivity and subjectivity. In the absence of any angels I intend boldly to step in. I remember a magnificent television programme called *The Mind of Man*. At one point we were shown experiments with sensors keyed to eye movements. It was shown that we do not see objects in the way a chemically operating camera takes a photograph, but more in the way a television camera scans the scene. We take soundings of the available visual data, integrating nodal points — such as the corners of a square — all in the twinkling of an eye (so to speak). This keys in neatly with the theory that children have reality expectations which are then met, or not, by their experience. If, for example, the baby's 'breast' expectation is not met, there will be throughout life a crippling attempt to manipulate reality into a latter-day analogue of that lost heritage. Now, could it be that there is an aural analogy of all this in the way that we understand the music we hear? Perhaps in any musical scale or cluster of notes, some notes, such as the top or bottom ones or mediant or melodic summit ones, define the conceptual matrix. Perhaps others fulfil an attention-directing function. In this category might be scalically organized notes, other than those already mentioned. Clearly the mediants will play a crucial rôle in defining whether we are in the major or the minor.

When the music is coming thick and fast, the time is short for us to sort out this multiplicity of information, and I dare say that we thus welcome any exaggeration of the signals. We do not then have to work so hard to make sense of what is happening.

With a portrait a likeness to the sitter is a *sine qua non*, but with a political cartoon in a hastily scanned newspaper, it is kind to the reader to exaggerate salient features of a politician's appearance. Cartoonists picked upon General de Gaulle's height and nose, and Harold MacMillan's coiffure and eyes, and thus they were immediately recognisable. My daughter has a toy which contains a wheel, half of which is coloured red and the other half blue. When the wheel is spun slowly the brain is still able to maintain its interpretation of what is being perceived as 'wheel, half red and half blue'. If one then speeds up the wheel progressively there comes a point when one can no longer hold this separation even if intellectually one knows that the wheel is still red and blue. The brain slips into a simpler mode, so to speak, and comes up with the interpretation 'purple wheel'. At high speeds the scales, in the absence of a touch of intonational exaggeration of the mediants and leading notes, will the sooner arouse the mental interpretation 'mongrel scales'!

Another aspect of creative intonation, whether considered statically, or, as we have just been doing, dynamically, might be called 'streamlining'. In mediaeval times, before we had the full panoply of accidentals, a note might be sung a semitone flatter than written if this would avoid tritones or otherwise 'streamline' a melody. This practice later became codified, and still later led to the accidentals, but let us realize that it arose from *musical intuition*. Experiment with:

*Ex. 228*

flattening the apogee (E♭), and sharpening the perigee (F♯). Relate your experiments to tempo.

However, in all this the greatest function of creative intonation is to make sure that we find the distinctive *personality* of each key. We must, as we play, know what the instantaneous key is. We must know the mediant and leading note, at very least, of that key, and the relationship of the instantaneous key to the tonic key of the piece. Only so can we bring out the dramatic unfolding of the modulations. A taxing task? Of course. Begin now and equip yourself with this sensibility. What is Bach playing without this sense of character, direction and harmonic turbulence?

One cannot bathe twice in the same river, and semanticists say that no word can encapsulate exactly the same meaning twice. I do not think it is too far-fetched that something of the same sort affects our attitude to intonation. The intonation of a note must vary according to its relationship to its melodic neighbours and the harmonic context.

Let us look at the beginning of the prelude from Bach's first solo suite in G major. Let us look at the varying rôle of the note B in the first four bars. In the first bar it is the mediant of the tonic and must be suitably intoned, sharper than the equal temperament B. It must also be magnetized upwards because of the aspirant quality of the melody at this point. In the second bar the B is the leading note of the subdominant and is pulled up into close relationship with it, conceivably sharper than the B in the first bar. In the third bar the B plays the rôle of a passing-note. In the fourth bar the B is again the mediant of the tonic, but here there is a noticeable relaxation and the B would thus be infinitesmally flatter than in the first bar. In the first bar we can say that we have a G major *in posse* whereas in the fourth bar we have it verily *in esse*, and indeed that is the whole point of these introductory four bars. In the fifth bar the B puts on the mantle of the fifth of the relative minor of the piece. So here, in short order, we have five different Bs! I need not emphasize that I am talking about subtleties.

So far, so good, but we are not out of the wood yet. If we take the first four bars of this prelude we get the progression:

*Ex. 229*

If we play the notes simultaneously as chords, we are constrained to such intonation as will permit fundamentals and partials to live harmoniously together. Now, clearly, if we then redeploy these chords in the way Bach did, the *basis* of the intonation will be the same, but it remains somewhat static, with no evolution. We have remarked the reason for the disparate semitones of the top line – the Bs are different, and so, indeed, are the Cs; but consider the middle line. Surely it is the upper tetrachord of the G major scale, and our earlier considerations (large tones, sharp leading-note), must have their say. Now it may seem curious that what is harmonically intolerable can be sometimes contrapuntally desirable! Thus we can go a long way towards full deployment of those aspects of creative intonation that pertain to simple melodies. But as always, theory must bow to practicalities and sound instinct.

Some players are surprised when they are playing double-stopping with contrapuntal implications that they encounter unsuspected difficulties. This is, I think, because they suffer a split between that mental position which desires equitemperence and an instinct which abhors it. Relativity in intonation is felt to be a threat to terra firma!

Let us consider the short cadenza in the Dvořák B minor concerto, second movement.

*Ex. 230*

1 The minim B must be sensitive to the changing demands of the harmonic undertow; G major, B major, E minor and G major.
2 Mediants must be high in the third crotchet beat of the first bar.
3 In the second bar the B must be sensitive to the changing demands of D and G, and so forth throughout the bar.

This is, in any case, a complicated passage. One has to think carefully as to which strand should at any moment predominate.

A very clear example of the need for pitch-variation in the same note repeated is to be found in Elgar's concerto, in the last movement at no. 68. The determinants to be taken into consideration are both melodic and harmonic. The Bb in the first bar is merely a passing note and can be played in equitemperamental relationship with its neighbours B and A, but the Bb in the next bar belongs to another harmonic planet. Both for harmonic and melodic reasons this note should be considerably flatter than its predecessor.

Before you start experimenting with this, may I issue a warning? One must be prepared to play a different intonation when rehearsing a concerto with the unyielding piano from that used when playing the same work with the orchestra. Be advised that in the latter case the string section will accommodate your eccentricities with goodwill and sensitivity, but do not presume the same qualities in the woodwind, let alone the brass. Get acquainted with the intonational problems of the blowing instruments. You may be partnered with one, and no prizes are awarded for showing up their shortcomings, indeed any misalliance will probably be blamed upon you — rightly so, for if we are not prepared to traffic with and in reality, we are not prepared, *tout court*.

Thus, for example, again in the Dvořák slow movement, four bars before no. 8 you are diminuendoing on a B one octave below the flute. Now some flautists find it difficult to execute a diminuendo without dropping the pitch progressively. Be alert and prepared to cover up the crime by joining in its commission! Another factor here is that one of the clarinets is also playing a B very quietly and may be getting to the end of his tether!

An interesting point arises in Shostakovich's Opus 40 sonata, in the two bars before no. 9 in the first movement. Any 'cellist who still thinks that these six Bs should remain unchanged is clearly beyond redemption! The accompaniment is masterly, not only in the harmony but also in the layout. It is almost as if Shostakovich, not himself a string-player, I would say, judging from his five- rather than four-fingered note grouping, nevertheless sensed that the 'cellist would want to increase tension and sharpen intonation up to the C major resolution. This C major chord begins to impose its authority well before its actualization.

If you are in a mood to experiment, try different intonations at no. 44 in the third movement. In the second bar, for example, would you choose an intonation for the Ab that 'goes' with both chords, or would you modify the intonation as the harmony changes? If so would you sharpen or flatten?

What of intonation in atonal music? I believe that if atonal music were to be made compulsory, tonal music being banned, string playing would be finished in a very short time. I believe that the theories I have put forward are assented to inwardly by all sensitive string players, although they might very well repudiate the terms in which I have expressed them. I believe that atonal music, *from the point of view of the performer*, is cybernetically unsound, and that in performing it we may well be guilty of some sort of *trahison des clercs*.

However, there is sanity in all insanity if one knows where to look and if one possesses the requisite codebook. When your ordinary, that is to say, extraordinary, string-player plays atonal music he is in the position of a sane man of goodwill confronted by madness. Recall, if you will, Chesterton's insight to the effect that the crazy man has not lost his reason: he has lost everything but his reason. Reason, *sans* instinct, *sans* insight, *sans* intuition, *is* madness. Our sane musician tries to make sense of this welter of craziness. I think that what he does is to treat the stuff as a music that proceeds by constant and instantaneous modulation. I think that he relates all the intervals to an intuitively postulated tonal centre, however evanescent. The elusiveness, not to say absence, of such a tonal centre is directly related to the ephemerality of the ego which is found in schizophrenia, but I deny that what Hindemith called 'dodecacophony' is *therefore* the music of our time. I say rather that it accurately expresses the diseased component of the modern soul. Its apparent vitality is that of a cadaver artificially and hideously kept alive by massive infusions of public money!

Our musician of goodwill will naturally want to throw off the strait-jacket of equitemperance, and will do so according to his sense of the fleeting tonal centre and to his intuition as to the composer's mood. Whether music that hovers from mood to whim to caprice is worth all the trouble, is perhaps arguable.

The theory of atonality, serialized or not, postulates equitemperance. True intonation, as we have seen, destroys this basis.

I hope I have introduced you to Creative Intonation in such a way that will tempt you to a lifetime's fascinating experimentation. I hope I have caused you to look at your 'cello with new eyes, and to listen to it with newly opened ears, to find in it endless hitherto unsuspected delights, both intellectual and sensuous. Apart from this feast of pleasure I am convinced that it is the 'open sesame' to good intonation from the purely functional standpoint. A positive plan is bound to win the day rather than that attitude so superbly caricatured by Chaplin in *Modern Times*, mindlessly tightening screws on a conveyor-belt.

# *Harmonics*

The Greeks knew that strings can be persuaded to vibrate in modes other than the fundamental (total vibration), and that there are simple mathematical ratios which relate those modes one to another. Naturally, being human, they were unable to resist the temptation to extrapolate this into a metatheology, putting to death the discoverer of irrational numbers!

A string vibrating totally has one antinode and two nodes, thus:

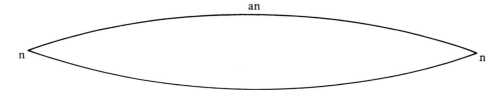

If we lightly touch the string at the half-way point we introduce a third node, thus forcing the string to adopt partial vibration, the string now oscillating in two halves, with two antinodes. The frequency is twice the fundamental, or, as we musicians say, an octave above.

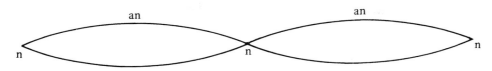

The string can also be persuaded to vibrate in other partial modes giving rise to the full harmonic series:

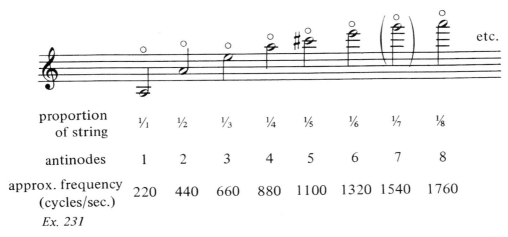

| proportion of string | $\frac{1}{1}$ | $\frac{1}{2}$ | $\frac{1}{3}$ | $\frac{1}{4}$ | $\frac{1}{5}$ | $\frac{1}{6}$ | $\frac{1}{7}$ | $\frac{1}{8}$ |
|---|---|---|---|---|---|---|---|---|
| antinodes | 1 | 2 | 3 | 4 | 5 | 6 | 7 | 8 |
| approx. frequency (cycles/sec.) | 220 | 440 | 660 | 880 | 1100 | 1320 | 1540 | 1760 |

*Ex. 231*

If we take the natural harmonics (partial vibrations) of the four strings, omitting the 'out-of-tune' ones, we find that we have quite a sackful of notes to play with. Remember that, apart from the first partial vibration (half-string-length, three nodes), these harmonics appear either side of the half-string-length node, a circumstance that will later be seen to be very convenient.

String length $\frac{1}{2}$ $\frac{1}{3}$ $\frac{1}{4}$ $\frac{1}{5}$ $\frac{1}{6}$ $\frac{1}{8}$

*Ex. 232*

The denotation of harmonics is not always as clear as it might be. A small 'o' over a note denotes either an open string or a note in the 'upper' (pitchwise) half of the instrument touched lightly and sounding at the same pitch as would be obtained by fully stopping the string at the same place. When the note is to be obtained by lightly touching the 'lower' (pitchwise) half of the instrument then a small ' ◊ ' is used to denote the *place* where the finger is to be put. Observe that this does *not* denote the pitch of the sounding note. I am always grateful to those composers and publishers who indicate precisely the sounding note they wish to be heard. Thus:

*Ex. 232*

## Exercises in natural harmonics

*Exercises in natural harmonics*

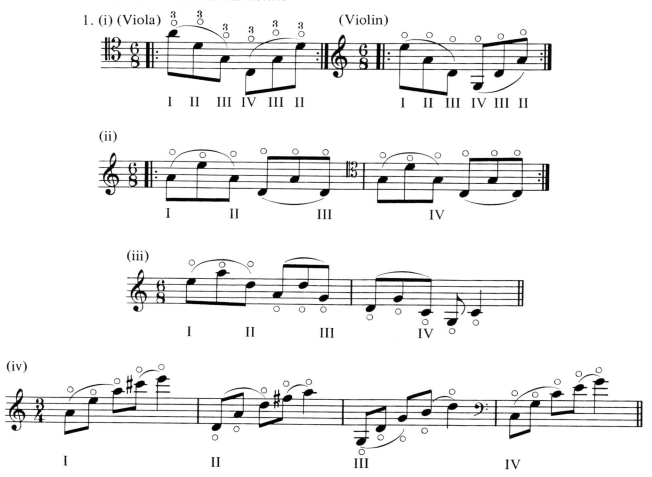

Ex. 233

Repeat the exercises using 2, 1, 4 or ♀, or pairs of fingers.

In 1. (iv) above you will have encountered a problem that must be made conscious. The gesture of the left hand arm unit is one of decreasing speed, whereas that of the right-hand arm unit may well be of constant or indeed increasing speed. How crucial again will be the total body-use and balance. That this is a practical matter will become apparent when we tackle the second movement of Shostakovich's Sonata Opus 40.

Ex. 234

An alternative way of playing this passage has certain advantages. At all events it makes a useful study:

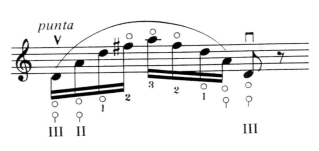

*Ex. 235*

2. Practise with, and without, vibrato:

Sul I

Sul II

Sul III

Sul IV

3. (i)

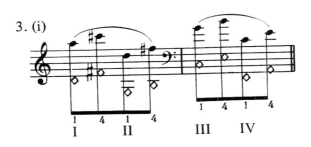

(ii)

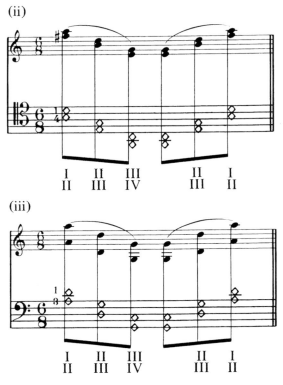

(iii)

*Ex. 236*

It is perfectly possible to vibrate the harmonic and the artificial harmonic. In a slow-moving theme at high pitches it can be helpful to put the thumb underneath the fingerboard. I have in mind especially the last note of Max Bruch's *Kol Nidrei*. (This technique can also be helpful in other contexts, e.g. the slow movement of Shostakovich's Opus 40 sonata.)

Artificial harmonics are made when we substitute a finger or thumb for the top nut, rather in the manner of the guitarist's *capotasto*. This clearly affords many new possibilities. It is important to keep the finger or thumb that is taking the rôle of the *capotasto* firmly down on the string, whilst the harmonic-making finger touches lightly.

The most frequently encountered mode for producing the artificial harmonic is that wherein the lightly touched note is placed a fourth above the firmly stopped one.

*Ex. 237*

This produces the double-octave above the 'firm' note and is quite comfortable to play. It is especially easy to conceptualize in that the lay of the hand is along one side of the thumb-positions grid (see p. 65, above). Artificial harmonic playing therefore has much in common with octave playing. An extended passage is to be found in Saint-Saëns A minor concerto. Play it with a little vibrato.

*Ex. 238*

The disadvantage of maintaining the ♀, 3 conformation is that all movement proceeds by *portamento*, so to speak. This can be mitigated by varying the upper finger:

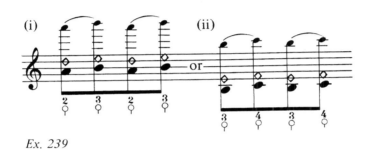

*Ex. 239*

The second example provides a good solution, mixed with natural harmonics, of the passage at no. 57 in Shostakovich's Opus 107 concerto (second movement). A subtle refinement here would be the judicious use of a touch of syllabic diminuendo (vol. 1, p. 90) to point up the conversation with the celeste. Naturally no attempt will be made to 'impersonate' the celeste.

I discovered that it is possible to force certain harmonics to speak without the usual preconditions being satisfied. Thus we can in fact execute trills, turns and grace notes which otherwise would entail unacceptably grotesque gyrations.

*Ex. 240*

Here is the beginning of 'Pe Loc' from Bartók's *Roumanian Dances*, in my arrangement:*

---

\* I use the sign 🎵 for two discrete notes taken in the same bow, the bow stopping between them. I use 🎵 for two notes taken in the same bow, the bow being lifted before both notes.

*Ex. 241*

I believe that much more can be done with such techniques than has so far been attempted, but composers must be warned to take advice before proceeding.

Although the customary conformation with artificial harmonics is a fourth between the 'firm' note and the lightly touched one, other intervals also produce acceptable sounds and have their place in the technique, either separately or mixed with those we have been studying. Thus:

*Interval of a fifth:*

*Ex. 242*

The Bartók excerpt translated:

*Ex. 243*

Some 'cellos appear to prefer the fourth-based artificial harmonic, others, the fifth-based ones. Hand size also is a determining factor.

*Interval of a major sixth:*

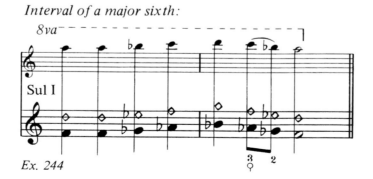

*Ex. 244*

## Mixing these three modes of artificial harmonic

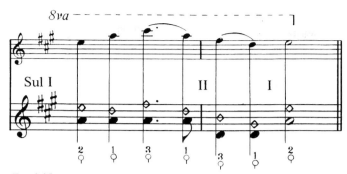

*Ex. 245*

## A short study in harmonics

*Ex. 246*

The harmonic can be played pizzicato, with or without vibrato, to fine effect.

There is a shifting technique which employs the harmonic as a 'stepping stone' so to speak. Consider the following:

*Ex. 247*

The third note starts firmly stopped but continues as a harmonic whilst the thumb seeks the neck of the instrument and operates as a pivot for the hand movement. All fingers can employ this technique, ♀ 0 presumably being pronounced 'thumbty'!